T0367826

50 Ways

to

Leave your 50's

50 Ways
to
Leave your 50's

SCOTT LUDWIG

50 WAYS TO LEAVE YOUR 50'S

Copyright © 2015 Scott Ludwig.

All rights reserved. No part of this book may be used or reproduced by any means, graphic, electronic, or mechanical, including photocopying, recording, taping or by any information storage retrieval system without the written permission of the publisher except in the case of brief quotations embodied in critical articles and reviews.

iUniverse books may be ordered through booksellers or by contacting:

iUniverse
1663 Liberty Drive
Bloomington, IN 47403
www.iuniverse.com
1-800-Authors (1-800-288-4677)

Because of the dynamic nature of the Internet, any web addresses or links contained in this book may have changed since publication and may no longer be valid. The views expressed in this work are solely those of the author and do not necessarily reflect the views of the publisher, and the publisher hereby disclaims any responsibility for them.

Any people depicted in stock imagery provided by Thinkstock are models, and such images are being used for illustrative purposes only. Certain stock imagery © Thinkstock.

ISBN: 978-1-4917-6097-0 (sc)
ISBN: 978-1-4917-6098-7 (e)

Print information available on the last page.

iUniverse rev. date: 02/18/2015

DEDICATION

To my son Justin, a constant reminder I'm getting older;
and my grandson Krischan, who helps me to forget.

FOREWORD

In 2013 I tried something I've never done before: I wrote every single day of the year. I ultimately published those 'chronological chapters' in two books (*My Life: Buy the Book* Parts 1 and 2) that quite honestly could have been broken down into four books since they totaled well over 1,000 pages. But since hindsight is 50-50, what's done is gone and there's no use in crying over water under the bridge *(I suck at clichés, incidentally)* I looked ahead to 2014 and realized I would soon be doing something else I've never done before: Turning 60. On December 10, 2014 to be exact.

But anyone can be 60…or at least anyone who has the health, desire and good fortune to last six decades on this planet can. *'So,'* I thought to myself, *'what other thing could I do in 2014 that I've never done before?'*

Then it hit me. Why not do 50 things I've never done before as a tribute to leaving the 50's behind? Not like the 50 things you might find on the lists of someone like Tiger Woods (win a 19th major championship, buy Nike) or Richard Branson (find Sasquatch, buy Planet Earth) of course, but 50 things I—with limited means and abilities—could do while maintaining a full time job and keeping up with everything that crossed my path as a husband, father, grandfather, homeowner, writer, runner and cat wrangler (my wife Cindy and I have five).

Fifty things I've never done before…within reason, of course. It's not like I was going to strip naked and run free in the middle of nowhere or anything. *(Let's try this again.)* It's not like I was going to build a spaceship and fly to the moon or anything. *(There, much better.)*

Now that 2014 is over I can honestly say it's been a lot of fun. As you'll find out in the pages ahead Cindy and I moved to the country after having lived in various cities for all of our lives. Best move we ever made. Just this morning a little after 4 a.m. as I was running along a country road near our new home in Senoia, Georgia a truck pulled up alongside me and stopped. The woman driving said she admired my dedication (apparently she's seen me more than once—I've run pretty much the same time and route since we moved here a little less than six months ago) and really appreciated seeing me each morning on her way to work. Do you know how many times that happened to me in the 36+ years I lived in the city? Let me think for a minute. I've got it: *NEVER!*

Like I said earlier: Moving to the country was the best move we ever made.

It's also one of the 50 things I'd never done before that you'll be reading about in this book. As for the other 49, you'll just have to keep reading and find out for yourself.

Scott Ludwig
January 13, 2015 (6:32 a.m.)
Senoia, Georgia

CONTENTS

CHAPTER 1

No Effing Way

—∞∞∞—

Swear off Profanity

I thought I'd start the year with something I've never truly done; something I thought would be relatively simple to do requiring very little effort or thought to accomplish. You know, something simple like picking the low-hanging fruit, shooting fish in a barrel or getting a degree from the University of Georgia. How hard could it possibly be to stop swearing for the next 365 days and finally fulfilling the one resolution that--year after year, I just can't seem to keep? I mean, if I put my heart and soul into it and gave an honest effort to refrain from saying anything I'd be embarrassed to say in front of my grandmother (God rest her soul), then surely doing it for a mere 12 months couldn't be that difficult, could it? Well, let's give it a try and find out.

January 1 - Cindy and I had just spent the long New Year's holiday with her two brothers and their wives at a cabin in the mountains of North Carolina. We would be driving the three-and-a-half hours back to our home in Peachtree City after I returned from my morning run. I headed out at 6:45 a.m. to run a hilly eight-mile course in a robust 24 degrees. The initial Arctic blast of icy cold fresh air caused me to mumble a couple of S-bombs to myself in the first 200 yards; I immediately wondered if I had already broken my resolution not to swear. I decided that since no one was awake within 10 miles of me--let alone within earshot--I hadn't broken my

1

resolution since no one heard anything I said (I'm using the 'If no one hears a tree falling in the forest, did it make a sound?' analogy). Once I got back to the cabin I quickly packed my bags, showered, loaded the car and waited silently and not-so-patiently but no one could tell because, like I already said I'm waiting silently and the best way to ensure I don't swear is to be absolutely quiet. I carry on my silence once we were (finally!) in the car and heading home and considered a few subjects for casual conversation. I ultimately rejected every one of them in my mind because I had a very strong opinion on every single one of them and suddenly realized that when I verbalize strong opinions is when there is the highest probability of me using an S-bomb, an F-bomb or the worst of them all, the dreaded GD-bomb. I have a tendency to use them as adverbs or adjectives. For example most people would say a runner is 'very fast;' I'm prone to call that same runner 'F-bombing fast.' (I'll stop here; I doubt you need any more examples.)

So I made it all the way home with my resolution still intact. So far so good: Only eight more hours until bedtime and I could say I made it through an entire day without swearing.

Around 3:00 p.m. Cindy asks me how much of the pound cake is still left on the cake plate in the kitchen. I removed the glass cover and as I set it down on the counter it banged against a large dish, made a loud CLINK that had I heard blindfolded I would have expected to hear the sound of shattered glass next. Fortunately nothing broke. I told Cindy there was still pound cake left and replaced the glass cover. Around 6:00 p.m. we finished our dinner and as I was taking the dirty plates to the sink Cindy asked me to get her a piece of pound cake. I walked over to the counter, removed the glass cover and as I set it down: **CLINK!** Two seconds after it happened I'm saying a silent prayer because once again nothing was broken (that's the good news). However, one second prior to *that* I said perhaps the **loudest GD-bomb** in quite a few years. Remember me saying the GD-bomb was the worst of the lot? Well, the look on Cindy's face (keep in mind she knew nothing of my commitment to keeping my 'no swearing' resolution this year) said it all: A combination of 'Same old Scott' and 'It just KILLS me when he says that!' Translation: LOO-ZER!

'It's a good thing I kept my resolution to myself,' I thought to myself. If only I could keep my swearing to myself. I walked into the living room and saw the Georgia Bulldogs force a turnover against Nebraska, giving them hope of pulling out a victory in the Gator Bowl. 'S-bomb,' I yelled. (Surprise! I hate Georgia.) Cindy barely noticed; after all it's just the same old Scott doing what he does best.

Tomorrow is another day. Surely I've learned from my mistakes.

Then again tomorrow is the day I am returning to work after being off for six days, a recipe for disaster. This might get ugly.

January 2 – I headed out the front door for my run at 4:10 a.m. It was not only cold; it was raining as well. I hate it when I have to start my run in a driving rain, especially when I'm leaving a warm, dry house behind. 'S-bomb,' I muttered to myself aloud for no one to hear but me, all the time remembering the falling tree in the forest from yesterday. I finished my run, shaved and showered (in that order; not the more commonly-said 'showered and shaved') and got dressed, impressed that over two hours had passed and I hadn't said any naughty words except for those couple of initial volleys when I left the house for the first time. I woke Cindy before I left, intentionally avoided any sort of dialogue that might encourage the use of colorful adjectives and headed to work. I rode in the car, listening to the '70's station and being alone with my thoughts when some a**clown in front of me waits until the last minute to move over one lane into the turning lane and caused ME to slam on my brakes and wait until someone allowed the a**clown to pull in front of them. As I always do when this occurs, I laid on the horn until I was able to move again. When I finally could I pulled up beside the a**clown and again, as I always do when this occurs, I looked him in the eye and shouted 'F-bombing a**hole.' Naturally with the windows up (it's raining, remember) the a**clown (a**clown, a**hole—same person; sorry if I confused you) couldn't hear me (falling tree number two); I had now gone a total of about two-and-a-half hours since waking up without uttering a bad word; at least not one that anyone else had heard.

Yet.

I called my supervisor on my cell phone to see how the day was shaping up. Although it's the day after a two-day holiday, we're going to be busy: *Very* busy, in fact. The kind of busy my supervisors and I are accustomed to calling 'F-bomb me' busy. This was going to be one of those days and as God is my witness I never stood a chance of not swearing: The words just flew out of my mouth. *'F-bomb me.'* The split second I spoke those two words I realized what I had done. The next word, in retaliation for my slip of the tongue: *'S-bomb.'*

Realizing the day was already a total loss for my new resolution, I spent the next 10 hours using my regular colorful assortment of adverbs and adjectives, with the intention of making January 3 the beginning of the new me.

After all, tomorrow is another GD-bomb day.

January 3 – I woke up at 3:30 a.m. to outside temperatures in the mid-20's and a wind chill that made it feel like it was in the teens. I drank my morning coffee and walked through the laundry room so I could get my running shoes out of the garage. When I opened the door to the garage I was hit in the face with an Arctic blast similar to the one a couple of mornings ago, causing me to mumble 'it's f-bombing cold' under my breath, knowing I had 'the falling tree' in my back pocket. But then I noticed Morgan the cat in her litter box out of the corner of my eye, looking at me with disappointed eyes and making an audible 'tsk tsk' for my poor vocabulary choice. That surprised me, mainly because I had no idea Morgan was in the laundry room at the time but also because apparently even *she* disapproved of me using an F-bomb.

Three strikes, I'm GD-bomb out. I surrender. Profanity: You win.

POSTSCRIPT: For those of you with a similar condition I did a little research and found various suggestions for breaking the habit of using words you wouldn't want your grandmother to hear. Things like:

- Recognize that swearing does damage.
- Start by eliminating casual swearing.
- Think positively.
- Practice being patient.
- Stop complaining.
- Use alternative words.
- Think of what you should have said.
- Blah blah and more blah.

It's almost as if someone actually believes some of that shit might actually work.

PARENTS: Should you use this story in the character development of your children, please have them reference the key below, as it explains the meaning of the abbreviations found in the preceding narrative:

- S-bomb = shoot
- GD-bomb = gosh darn
- F-bomb = fudge
- A** = apple
- Shit = shit

CHAPTER 2

All Bets are Off

⤬

Win the Office Betting Pool

In 1985 I started a pool at work for the NCAA Basketball Championship Tournament, better known as 'March Madness.' The first year we had seven participants. The winner was determined by the total number of tournament wins your five chosen teams had during the course of the tournament. There was a two-way tie for first place that initial year. They decided to split the pot; all $14 of it.

Over the years the popularity of the pool grew. One year the prize money (winner take all) amounted to $395, the biggest payout ever offered. A woman who entered for the first time—and selected her teams by virtue of the appeal of the names of their mascots—won. In 1988 'John' (maybe/maybe not his real name) picked the Kansas Jayhawks as one of his five teams. I distinctly remember mocking him mercilessly for picking the team with the most losses (11) in the field of 64 teams. Not only did Kansas win the tournament, 'John' won the pool. That was the day I had the confirmation I had been expecting: Betting Karma hates me. Last year was the 29ᵗʰ anniversary of the March Madness pool, and as you might expect I am oh-for-29.

I started another pool in 1985 as well: the NCAA College Football Bowl pool. The winner is determined by how many winning teams you can pick amongst all of the post-season bowl games. In the event of a tie there is a randomly chosen tiebreaker to determine the winner. In 1997 I was tied for the most wins heading into the final game of the year; we both selected Florida to beat Florida State in the Sugar Bowl. Florida won in convincing fashion, winning 52 – 20 so we had to resort to the tiebreaker to determine the winner, which was total passing yards for Florida's quarterback, Danny Wuerffel. My guess was 440; the other guy guessed somewhere around 300. After three quarters Wuerrfel had already thrown for 306 yards, well on his way to the 400-yard mark. However, Florida had a commanding lead entering the fourth quarter so the need for Wuerffel to pass was gone, he was taken out of the game and the other guy won the pool, proving once again Betting Karma hates me.

I decided this year things were going to change. After this year's bowl season Betting Karma would be kissing my ass: I was going to win the football pool and avoid matching my oh-for-29 record in the basketball pool. There was no way—NO WAY that I was going to be a composite oh-for-58 in the three decades of the two office betting pools.

After 33 bowl games I had 23 victories; the next closest person had 21. (I looked like a genius selecting Nebraska to beat Georgia in the Gator Bowl. Truth be known I hate Georgia so much I would never in a million years pick them to win *anything*. Then again I looked like an idiot for picking UNLV to beat North Texas. I wish I had taken the time to do a little research prior to making my selections; if I had I might have noticed that North Texas was favored over UNLV by something like a zillion points.) Regardless, even though I spent barely more than a minute selecting my 35 winners, I still had a two-victory lead with two games still to be played. I liked my chances.

My last two predicted winning teams were different than my rival, so I had three chances to win the pool: My team winning the 34th bowl game (Go Daddy Bowl; I picked Ball State; my rival Arkansas State), my team winning the 35th bowl game (the BCS Championship; I picked Auburn; my rival Florida State) or me winning the tiebreaker (total points in the championship game; I predicted 73 while my rival predicted 67).

Bowl game #34: Arkansas State beats Ball State 23 – 20. There goes my first chance of winning the pool, but not to worry: I still have two chances left. I feel as if I'm playing tennis and I have three match points and my opponent just fought off the first one.

Bowl game #35: Auburn against Florida State with the National Championship at stake. To win the pool I need Auburn to win. Should FSU win I need a minimum of 71 points scored in the game to win. Auburn takes a commanding 21 – 3 lead in the second quarter, but FSU closes the gap to 21 – 10 by halftime. In an exciting fourth quarter the lead changes hands several times until Auburn scores with 1:19 left in the game and pulls in front, 31 – 27. I won't need the tiebreaker: Auburn would win this game outright and I would win my first office betting pool since the days of Ronald Reagan and MTV! 'Turn the lights out, the party's over' as Dandy Don used to sing during the golden age of *Monday Night Football*. I thought the lyric was appropriate since this just so happened to be a Monday night, it was almost midnight and I was ready to turn the lights out and get to bed since I had an early alarm set for the following day (try 3:15 a.m. on for size).

But then…IT happened. Florida State made an incredible last-minute drive to score the go-ahead touchdown, taking a three-point lead and leaving a mere 13 seconds on the game clock for Auburn to retaliate. In other words, in another 13 seconds Betting Karma was going to kick me to the curb for the 60th time. Sure, my rival and I were tied with 23 bowl victories, but by virtue of the 65 total points in the game he won the tiebreaker.

I spent a restless 45 minutes or so in bed, finally falling asleep around 1 a.m. One-hundred-and-thirty-five minutes later my alarm reminded me I was a loser, and that it was now time for me to start preparing for this year's March Madness office pool. After all, Betting Karma will be ready to flex its muscles again by then and will be looking for its most dependable fall guy.

However, it wasn't a total loss as I had a 'first' I wasn't expecting: After only two hours and 15 minutes of sleep I went for a 10-mile run at 4 a.m.

in five-degree weather with a wind chill that lowered the temperature to a robust minus 10 degrees. I'm fairly certain I've never done that before and if there's a God other than Betting Karma I doubt I'll ever have to do it again.

Postscript: Later in the year I didn't win the March Madness office pool yet again, extending my lifetime record of futility to 0-30. I'd be lying if I said I was surprised, because I certainly wasn't.

CHAPTER 3

Quite a Stretch

---⊂∞⊃---

Take a Yoga Class

When I signed up for my first yoga class last month I was the first person to sign up. That made me a little concerned for two reasons: (1) The lone requirement for the course—other than the $27 registration was that 'students should be able to move from standing to the floor without assistance' and (2) if that is the only requirement for the course, how difficult could it possibly be? The class was taught by a young lady named Shelly and would meet from 6 to 7 p.m. on the four Tuesdays in January.

Here goes nothing.

Session # 1 – Loosening Up

I arrived 10 minutes early, half expecting to be told upon arrival that the class had been cancelled since I was the only person who registered for it. Once I entered the dimly-lit classroom and saw women in Spandex rolling their mats out on the floor—in perfectly straight lines and equidistant from one another, I knew this was going to happen: *I was taking a yoga class!* I placed my mat in the back corner of the classroom next to a window, the blinds closed to prevent anything outside the room from ruining the ambiance the instructor was trying to achieve. Shelly came over and introduced herself and asked what experience I had in yoga. I proudly said I had been doing some self-taught yoga on my living room floor for the past four months, thinking to myself what a stud I must be since I was way beyond moving from standing to the floor without assistance.

Shelly continued about her business, setting out what I'm pretty certain were strands of white Christmas lights around the perimeter of the room. She then placed an electronic candle next to everyone's mat; again, I'm assuming to lend to the ambiance she was trying to create.

I stood on my mat and did a few exaggerated Chubby Checker twists to loosen up, only to catch a glimpse of a woman in the back row wrapping one of her legs around the back of her head. In my mind I couldn't decide if she was being a complete showoff or a total bitch; instead I made a mental note not to look towards the back of the room for any reason whatsoever. I looked around the room and noticed that for every single mat on the floor there was a female in close proximity doing a lot better job of stretching than me. If it wasn't for the fact I knew Shelly—whom I knew to be the instructor of the class I signed up for because she had already introduced herself to me I would have thought I was in the wrong room.

You might remember a couple of sentences ago I specifically said *females* were in close proximity to their mats. That's because at that time I was the only male in the room. Imagine my relief when 'Mike' (may or may not be his real name, but he looks like his name would be 'Mike') rolled out his mat next to mine, thus shifting the balance of power more in my favor: Males in yoga class – 2; females in yoga class – 16. Whereas I had introduced myself earlier to Shelly as a runner, Mike introduced himself as a swimmer, right before introducing his wife, thus making me the only non-chaperoned male in the room.

Shelly took her spot at the front of the room. Notice how nonchalantly I wrote and equally nonchalantly you just now read that last sentence? That would be because you had to be there to realize *I had actually positioned my mat on the* **FRONT** *row!!* To say that I was intimidated would be an

understatement. I suddenly became so nervous, so self-conscious, so…
vulnerable.

> *'What's the worst that could happen?' I thought to my panic-stricken
> self. 'I could accidently fart…and there wasn't a single pet in the
> room I could blame it on. What if the women notice my socks in no
> way match the outfit I'm wearing? Will they compare my yoga form
> to that of the instructor, seeing as both of us are in their fields of
> vision? Sure, I made it from standing to the floor without assistance,
> but will I be able to get from floor to standing the same way?'*

The first thing Shelly asked us to do was lie on our back with one hand
on our stomach and one hand on our heart. Then she asked us to close
her eyes. It's rather obvious at this point Shelly doesn't know who she's
dealing with, because the next thing I know two minutes had passed (an
observation I made by looking at the clock on the wall) and she asked us
to get in the Downward Dog position.

> *There are three things you may have picked up in that last statement: (1)
> I fell asleep seconds after being asked to lie on my back; (2) for the first
> time in many years I was 'clock watching' and (3) Shelly assumed everyone
> knew the Downward Dog position (Note: All of us did, even the swimmer
> next to me who had never done any yoga in his life until tonight).*

For the next 58 minutes Shelly gave us non-stop instructions, doing all
of the yoga herself as she spoke. It was all I could do to *breathe* trying to
do all of the various poses and maneuvers she was putting us through, let
alone talk. The toughest one for me was lying on my stomach, arching my
body backward in the shape of a slice of watermelon, bending my legs at
the knees and grabbing both of my ankles with my hands. I found this one
the most difficult because of the fact I wasn't able to grab both ankles at
the same time. Right ankle? No problem. Left ankle? Big problem.

The next toughest for me was a tie between any and every pose requiring
me to balance on one leg. Let me be the first to tell you: Balance is not one
of my strong suits these days. As I mentioned earlier the room was dimly-lit
and I was positioned next to a window, and where there's a window there's

a wall. In other words I had the perfect storm for creating the *illusion* of balance. (Note to self: Be certain to secure the same spot next week. On the same note: Do not eat beans for lunch on Tuesday, give strong consideration to bringing my neighbor's dog to class and drop Shelly a hint that I'm about as flexible as a nail file—just so she knows.)

One down and three more to go. I'm willing to be patient and see how this thing plays out. After all, Rome wasn't built in a day.

Now if you'll excuse me, I need to locate my left ankle. I know it's back there somewhere.

Session # 2 – The Gumby Hour

The second 60-minute session (yes, I was still watching the clock) was exactly what a group of limber, bendable yogis was looking for. Everyone in class was as flexible and limp as a strand of spaghetti; I was no exception. There was only one problem: I was the only strand of spaghetti who didn't get to spend 12 minutes submerged in a pot of boiling water before class.

The non-stop regimen of bend this, bend that, put-your-left-hand-on-the-yellow-circle-and-your-right-foot-on-the-blue took its toll. At some point during the assault the instructor dropped a block on my mat as I was sweating profusely trying to touch the back of my head with one of my ankles. (Apparently the block—hard foam about the size of a brick--is used in yoga for practitioners to compensate for any physical limitations they may have. I wouldn't know, as my pride wouldn't let me stoop to such desperate measures.) A couple of minutes later the instructor passed by my mat again and nudged the block with her foot up against my side. However, I refused to admit defeat and continued trying to wrap my right leg over my left shoulder without that damn block. It wasn't long before she made a third pass by my mat, leaned over and whispered in my ear: 'Are you hurt?' 'No,' I replied. I lied. I would like to add that somehow, some way I also survived, blocks be damned.

Session # 3 – The Wallenda Hour

All that was required for the third 60-minute drill was some semblance of balance. Therein lies the first problem: When I was born and fell out of the Balance Tree I managed to miss every single branch on the way down. The second problem was that the balance portion of the program immediately followed 20 minutes of bending and stretching that pretty much sucked every ounce of energy out of both legs. So when the instructor had us on our feet the final 40 minutes of the evening—and by 'feet' I actually mean 'one foot at a time'—things got ugly. As you may remember I mentioned I had the good foresight at the very first session two weeks ago to place my mat next to the wall. Tonight that decision paid huge dividends. If not for the wall, I would have spent the last 40 minutes on my ass. (I wasn't kidding when I said I missed every single branch.) I heard Mike on the mat next to me being told by his wife the trick to maintaining balance was to focus your eyes on a specific spot on the wall. Let me be the first to say simply placing my left hand on a specific spot on the wall proved to be a viable, simpler and more effective alternative.

Interestingly enough, the next morning in my office I tried several of the balance poses I couldn't do during yoga class. I did all of them. Damn near flawlessly, if I do so say so myself. Game on: Bring on next week!

Session # 4 – The Grand Finale

Three inches of snow fell in the Atlanta area today. In other words, Atlanta came to a standstill. Yoga class wasn't immune to the standstill, evidenced by this Email I received from the instructor five hours before class:

Greetings, Yogi:

Due to the snow and the closing of the Kedron Facility we will not have practice tonight. My apologies to your hamstrings (she remembered!) *as they were on our agenda tonight!*

Tonight was to have been the last class of our January session.

February enrollment is open. Enjoy a few sun salutations
as you watch the snow fall. Stay warm and safe!

Namaste,

Shelly

February's yoga class will have to go on without me. I'll keep doing my yoga, but I'll do so in the privacy and safety of my living room.

That way the next time Atlanta is hit with three inches of snow, this particular yogi will be keeping his Namaste alive.

Whatever that means.

Postscript: I still do yoga about six days a week. Alone, in my own home and free to pass gas whenever the spirit moves me. Namaste.

CHAPTER 4

No Way Out

⟨∞⟩

Attend an Allman Brothers Concert

Last Christmas morning, once all the presents were opened Cindy leaned over to me and said there was one other thing she intended to give me: Concert tickets to see a tribute concert at Atlanta's Fabulous Fox Theater in January. An all-star lineup would be taking the stage to sing the words and play the music of the legendary Gregg Allman, a unique one time only event. However by the time Cindy called to purchase the tickets, the show had sold out. Cindy felt bad about it, but I felt even worse because I know how much she loves the Allman Brothers and had yet to see them perform in concert.

So you can imagine my excitement when my sister called me right around New Year's Day and asked if I'd be interested in getting a pair of tickets to *All My Friends: Celebrating the Songs and Voice of Gregg Allman.* It just so happened that Tom, a friend of hers had a pair of tickets available. At this point I was so excited about the prospect of getting the tickets I'm not exactly sure how Tom ended up having the tickets available. Hope might have said he landed a backstage pass, was asked to play with the band or was heading off to astronaut school; I can't say for sure because I wasn't really listening. All I heard was *I might get my hands on a pair of tickets to see the Allman Brothers Band!*

At Hope's request Tom gave me a call. Now get this: *He was willing to sell the tickets to me at face value!* I thought to myself that Tom must be really excited about getting a backstage pass/playing with the band/the prospect of traveling to outer space (I really need to listen better). Before I even put a check in the mail to pay for the tickets ($340 for the pair and before you even ask: Yes, that was face value) I had an Email from Tom with the tickets attached. What a great, trusting guy! If Tom didn't live in Washington D.C./on a spaceship I imagine one day we could be the best of friends.

On the night of the show we were hurrying along Peachtree Street to get to our seats by the advertised 7:30 p.m. start. People everywhere were asking if anyone had tickets for sale. It was all I could do to refrain from asking how much they were willing to pay, figuring I could come up with enough money for a 4X-HDTV if I ran into the right customer… or get arrested by an undercover policeman for scalping tickets because as you may already know karma hates me.

We get to our seats maybe five minutes early, giving us 35 minutes to dry off (it was a rainy night in Georgia) before the show finally gets underway around 8:00. There isn't a bad seat in the Fox (unless you end up sitting behind Alice the Goon or one of the Atlanta Hawks), but the instant the first note is played everyone in the house is standing and will remain that way for the next three-and-a-half hours until the show is over.

Gregg Allman's friends took the stage—one after another to sing and/or play with the talented session musicians on stage to perform some of the finest southern rock one could ever hope to hear. Maybe four or five songs into the show the song *No Way Out* got things smoking. No, I'm not referring to the music because the music had been smoking since the very first song. I'm referring to *smoking*, as in*mari-jay-wanna. It's the first time I've caught a whiff of 'the evil weed' in a concert since the '70's, a time when the *deed with the weed* warranted nothing more than a hand slap (from the law) or an a**-kicking (from your parents).

I trust this isn't a news flash for the Fox Theater management.

The musicians throughout the tribute were amazing and it was evident they all *wanted* to be there. The classiest comment I heard all night was from Trace Adkins. After singing *I'm No Angel* and *Trouble No More* he told the crowd: 'This is the coolest thing I've ever done in my career.' I'm no fan of country music by any stretch of the imagination, but I'm now a fan of Trace Adkins.

Some of my personal favorites of the night were Widespread Panic's rendition of *Just Ain't Easy*, Gregg Allman and Jackson Browne's duet on *Melissa*, Eric Church's performance of *Ain't Wastin' Time No More*, and every single note played by Allman Brothers Band guitarist Derek Trucks (that man can make a guitar cry for mercy). For me the highlight of the night was the Allman Brothers performance of *Whipping Post*, a 20-minute extravaganza illustrating the musical talents of each member of the band.

Other featured performers included former Allmans keyboardist Chuck Leavell (the girl sitting next to me said she shared a cab with him once) and Zac Brown (Cindy reminded me Zac Brown came into her store one time and spent quite a bit of money). I wanted to tell them both that I might possibly know one of the boys in the band (I couldn't be certain Tom was up there because we'd never met in person and I had no idea what he looked like, or if he was even on Planet Earth for that matter).

Rounding out the talent was Sam Moore (of Sam & Dave), Dr. John, Pat Monahan (Train front man), John Hiatt, Taj Mahal, Martina McBride and Vince Gill. (Speaking of Vince Gill, a woman I worked with in the '80's had a crush on him, always commenting on how good he looked in a pair of tight jeans. I imagine she might be surprised to see him now: His jeans were still tight all right, but the reasons were all wrong.) There were a couple of other musicians but I missed their performances because Cindy sent me to the lobby to buy her a beer and apparently the people at the concession stands were feeling the affects of whatever was in the air (mari-jay-wanna) because until tonight I had never seen anyone stone cold sober take three minutes to pour a glass of beer from a tap and even longer to make a mixed drink.

Towards the end of the night Gregg Allman was presented on stage with a pair of framed certificates for his life's work.

As for Cindy, who bought a copy of the Allman Brothers Band's double album *Eat a Peach* the day it was released back in 1972: She finally got to see one of her favorite bands of all time.

And me? Well, I just might be friends with an astronaut.

CHAPTER 5

Deep in Enemy Territory

―∞∞―

Get a Win at Auburn

This seemed like the perfect opportunity.

The Florida Gators basketball team had a record of 14 wins—including a perfect 3 – 0 in Southeastern Conference (SEC) games--and only 2 losses and were ranked 7th in the nation. Auburn's team was sporting a record of 8 wins and 6 losses (including a 19-point loss at home to Northwestern State) and was still winless in the SEC at 0 – 3. So when the schedule called for the Gators to play the Auburn Tigers it seemed like the perfect opportunity for me to visit Auburn, Alabama and leave as a winner for the very first time.

Up until now I was oh-for-Auburn. My first trip to War Eagle Country was in 1989 to see the Gator football team lose to the Tigers by a score of 10 – 7. Seventeen years later Cindy made the trip with me to Jordan-Hare Stadium. Before the game we found a parking lot at a local church that included parking, all-you-can-eat barbecue and all-you-can-drink beer for only $5. After parking the car, loading a plate full of barbecued chicken and potato salad and being handed an ice cold beer, I asked the woman taking my $5 bill if the pastor of the church knew what they were doing. Her reply: 'Who do you think handed you that beer?' Thank the Good

Lord for Southern Hospitality. Time out for a brief tally: Two trips to Auburn; two Gator losses: Auburn 27, Florida 17.

My third chance to grab a victory in Auburn was in 2011. Cindy and I watched the Tigers beat our Gators 17 – 6 in what could have been the worst college football game in history. If there were ever a game that neither team should have won, it was this one. Auburn's offense was anemic; the Gators' even worse. It was a minor miracle that Florida's offense even touched the ball, considering the Gators *fumbled five punts* during the game. I can remember the Gator football teams in the '80's having trouble fielding punts, but even at their worst five fumbled punts would constitute an entire season, not a single game. Cindy and I left the game a couple of minutes before it was over (a rarity for us) because we had a feeling things were going to turn ugly once the clock read :00. We hit that nail on the head, because after the game the Auburn fans were taunting us without mercy, chasing us to our car much in the same way the angry villagers chased after Frankenstein's monster with their pitchforks and burning torches in their hands.

So getting back to what I was saying earlier, I was oh-for-Auburn. If you factor in the Auburn Half Marathon I ran in 2010, well, I didn't win that either so at this point you can say I was oh-for-four in Tiger Town.

But today things were going to change. Cindy and I left our home in Peachtree City in plenty of time to make the 3:00 p.m. tip-off, especially since the game would start at 3:00 p.m. in the Central Time Zone. If you can grasp Cindy's propensity to be late you can appreciate me not letting her in on that little tidbit of time zone information until I parked the car across the street from the Auburn Arena about 90 minutes before game time. A bit peeved, Cindy asked me how long I had known that Alabama time was an hour behind Georgia time. I told her 'since about 7th grade,' which proved once again that her sense of humor and mine are in two different time zones as well.

I'll get to the outcome of the game in a moment. But first I have to tell you about the game within the game, or as Cindy and I call it our two hours in the Twilight Zone.

- First time out: Several hundred miniature parachuting cows fall from the rafters, a promotion from the local Chick-Fil-A. I noticed one boy running back-and-forth along a mostly deserted aisle with three cows in one hand and two in another; his sister in the row behind him with a handful of her own. I'm guessing with the number of free coupons (they were attached to the cows) they accumulated their parents didn't have to worry about dinners for the next week or so.

- Second time out: The cheerleaders scoured the crowd looking for the 'loudest fans,' easily discernible by any fan in the first couple of rows doing pseudo jumping jacks and shaking their heads and shoulders uncontrollably until a Domino's personal pan pizza was placed in their flailing hands to calm them down.

- Third time out: One lucky fan was given the chance to WIN A CAR! All she had to do was make a 94-foot putt from one side of the basketball court to the other. Moments after her putt ricocheted off the feet of the members of the press in the front row at courtside, the public address announcer commended her on her *GOOOOOD TRY.*

- Halftime: Two fans appeared at mid-court dressed as a pair of Michelin Men, their costumes so 'inflated' that their arms stuck out straight to their sides and their mobility was severely restricted. Their challenge: To engage in in a bout of 'sumo wrestling' with the winner to be determined by the first rikishi (sumo wrestler) to make their opponent fall to the floor twice. In an entertaining performance the red Michelin Man beat the blue Michelin Man two falls to one and enjoyed the spoils of victory: a gift bag from a prominent wireless service. I can only imagine how proud this would have made the Japanese, the Founding Fathers of sumo wrestling.

Them again, the parachuting cows and the Michelin Men couldn't hold a torch to the three 'fans' standing immediately behind Cindy and I. As far as we could tell, two of them were Auburn fans and two of them were Florida fans. Why we had a hard time identifying their school affiliations will be evident once you become familiar with some of their dialogue we overheard during the game. I'll give them nicknames so you can keep score at home:

Basketball Savant (BS): The Gators are the ones in the blue uniforms.
Grasshopper #1: Is Auburn in white?
BS: Yes; wearing white makes them the home team.
Grasshopper #2: What does Florida wear when they're the home team?
BS: Orange. Sometimes white, it just depends.
Grasshopper #3: *Tweeeeeyht. Tweeeeeyht.* (Annoying sound similar to the sounds the smoke detector in our house made the last time I burned something in the microwave)

BS: That player just got fouled in the act of shooting.
Grasshopper #1: What happens now?
BS: He shoots two free throws. They count for one point if he makes them.
Grasshopper #2: What if he got fouled trying a three point shot?
BS: He can shoot as many as three free throws, but he only gets to shoot as long as he keeps making them. If he misses the first one, he's done.
Grasshopper #3: (After the first free throw is made) *Tweeeeeyht. Tweeeeeyht.*

BS: Billy Donovan just called a time out.
Grasshopper #1: What did he do that for?
BS: Some of the players need some Gatorade. They're getting tired from running up and down the court and Gatorade gives them fresh legs.
Grasshopper #2: Is that why the players are sitting on folding chairs while the coach is talking to them?
BS: Now you're catching on.

Grasshopper #3: (As the Gators are drinking from their Gatorade bottles)
Tweeeeeyht. Tweeeeeyht.

Yep, these guys had about as much business being at a basketball game as I do being at a science fair. *(Believe me, if you knew me better you'd be in stitches right about now.)* I was shocked when I turned around after the game was over and saw these four fans looked to be in their late 30's. Judging by their ongoing dialogue for the past 40 minutes I would have sworn they were at some age where they may not have had too much exposure to the game of basketball at this point in their lives.

As for the game, Florida was fortunate to leave Auburn Arena with a 68 – 61 win, considering they did it without any noticeable contribution from any of their guards. From what I've seen of the Gators so far this season, it was one of their poorest efforts. But a win is a win.

Or as the Basketball Savant said about the play of the Gator guards: 'The smaller players' job is to dribble the ball up and down the court and give the ball to the bigger players so they can make the baskets. That's why you don't see Florida's smaller players scoring many points.'

Postscript: The Gators went on to finish their season as the first team to finish with a perfect record of 18 – 0 in Southeastern Conference games. They went on to win three games in the Conference Tournament, defeating Kentucky in the Championship Game. It was the third time Florida beat Kentucky this season; I mention it so that when you read 'The Calipari List' near the end of this book you'll know how much beating Kentucky three times meant to me.

CHAPTER 6

The Emperor's New Shoes

———— ⟨∞⟩ ————

Run in a Pair of Hokas

Of all the things I knew prior to January 1st that I wanted to do for the first time this year, none caused me more anxiety, more apprehension or more cause for deliberation than what I did today.

I'm making a special notation in my running log to mark the occasion: January 25, 2014 - *I finally ran in my Hokas.*

You see, I've had my pair of size-10 Hoka One One's (that would be the official name of the shoes) in their original box in my closet since September.

September of 2012.

So you may be wondering why they're making their first appearance today.

What can I say? I like to live on the edge, and what better time to run in Hokas for the first time than 2014, my Year of Living Dangerously.

Let me back up for a moment. I've been having a variety of physical ailments and impairments ever since running, walking and crawling 100 miles through some God-forsaken mountain range in California in the summer of 2006. (Fact #1: When it comes to running in the mountains, I am a fish out of water. Fact #2: If a fish remains out of water too long it will die. Fact #3: I believe you see my point.) Since that particular race I've been on a yet unfulfilled quest to find the 'perfect running shoe' to absorb the punishment I subject my body to as I continue to run every single day.

A couple years ago I heard more and more runners commenting on how much they loved running in their Hokas. They were the new kid on the running shoe block and everyone wanted to jump on the bandwagon. I began asking the runners I saw wearing Hokas what they thought of them, and without exception they were all huge fans. I saw more and more of them on the feet of runners of all shapes and sizes at various races. According to the favorable reviews I was reading and hearing, Hoka running shoes were living up to its company slogan: *Time to fly.*

So after giving it more thought than ever before about buying a pair of running shoes, I broke down and ordered a pair of Hokas online. The caveat was the cost: $169. Running shoe experts will tell you to expect 500 – 600 miles from a pair of running shoes. Doing the math, it appears it would be cheaper to drive a HumVee 500 miles rather than run 500 miles in a pair of Hokas. At that price the One One's better do everything I dreamed of, if not more. At the very least I expected them to make me feel like I'm running along a path covered by a layer of cotton balls; best case scenario they make me feel like I'm running on a cloud.

This morning, after spending the last 16 months in my closet the Hokas found their way onto my feet for the very first time. I opened the shoebox—large enough to hold a toaster oven—and my One One's finally saw the light of day. *(That's a lie. It was 5:00 a.m. and even when my run was over the sun still hadn't made an appearance. Word of caution: I'm prone to lie at the drop of a hat.)*

'What an odd creature,' I thought to myself. *(Actually I said it out loud and our orange tabby Moe, who was sleeping in the chair I was sitting on the edge of to put on the Hokas, thought I was talking to him. I already told you I'm prone to lie at the drop of a hat; perhaps now you believe me.)*

The white pair of Hokas sported HUGE heels that brought back memories of the white platform shoes I wore to my senior prom some four decades ago. There was an extra pair of shoelaces in the box but for the life of me I don't know why because the shoes featured an intricate lacing system where the laces are threaded through a plastic gizmo that gives way to a leather whatchamacallit and I couldn't see how the shoelaces could be removed since they actually formed one big loop with no loose ends. (There wasn't an instruction manual in the shoebox; by all rights there should have been.) Through a couple minutes of trial and error, I did manage to figure out how to tighten the shoelaces (it involved separating the blue and the gray halves of the plastic gizmo and pushing them back together once the laces felt snug).

At 5:30 Al and I headed out for our regular Saturday morning run. It was 16 degrees with a wind chill bringing the temperature down into single digits. I took my first couple of steps…and I can most definitely assure you I was not running on clouds. Not even a path covered in cotton balls. I remembered one of the runners I asked about Hokas telling me it took three or four runs until you could truly appreciate their performance. Three miles into my run I heard the familiar 'clap' as my right foot struck the asphalt. 'When will it be my Time to Fly?' I thought to myself. *(Again I lie. I actually directed this question to Al, who had no earthly idea what I was talking about.)*

> *We interrupt this message for a brief public service announcement.*
> *If you're running in expensive running shoes and stop on the side*
> *of the road to answer nature's call on a dark, cold and very windy*
> *morning it is highly advisable to do so with your back to the wind.*
>
> *We now return to our regularly scheduled message.*

So after my first 10 miles running in a pair of Hokas, I'm disillusioned, disappointed and just a little bit disgusted. Not as disillusioned, disappointed or disgusted as when I ran in a pair of Sketcher Go Run's *(Can you say 'goodbye shins?')* for the first time, but pretty darn close.

Sure, I'll give them a few more tries in the next few weeks; after all I did invest $169 in them. But for now I have to go.

It's Time to Cry.

Postscript: I wear my Hokas regularly, just not to run in because that would be crazy. Not paying $169-for-a-pair-of-running-shoes crazy, but close.

CHAPTER 7

Kind of a Drag

———— ∞ ————

Drag Race

The day started off peaceful enough. Another day at the office pretty much like any other, except today was the day for our annual Super Bowl luncheon with one of our company vendors to break up the day. Personally I was looking forward to relaxing with the vendor's representatives and my Porsche employees as we compared notes and talked trash about the upcoming Big Game.

Let me back up for a second. The vendor's President drives a white 2008 Porsche Boxster. When I met with him last year he drove it to my place of employment and when I saw it I really liked the color, so much that when I ordered my next company car I ordered one just like it. We had agreed to drive our white sports cars the next time we saw one another: Today was that day.

At lunch everyone was sitting around enjoying lunch in our large meeting room when the vendor representative got in front of my employees and told them how much he appreciated our business, the same as he had done for the past several years. Everything was fine up to that point; until he continued talking, that is.

'I'd like to introduce you to our President, Mr. Eric _____. I'm sure you noticed he's driving one of your products; in fact the same model as your boss Scott. After lunch we have a little entertainment lined up for you. Eric and Scott will be racing one another in the parking lot to see who has the fastest Boxster.'

'That's news to me,' I thought to myself. 'I thought Eric and I were going to be racing each other on FOOT,' I said out loud, hoping the humorous intent would hide the fact that I was suddenly scared shitless on several levels: (1) I've never drag raced in my life; (2) What if the police swing by while we're engaging in illegal activity? (3) If I decline the challenge my employees will think I'm a coward; (4) My employees are counting on me to defend the honor of our company and I can't let them down; and (5) I'VE NEVER DRAG RACED IN MY LIFE!!!

At this point I still had one piece of pizza left. I recalled my mom telling me a long time ago to chew everything 23 times before swallowing; how odd the thought crossed my mind at that exact moment. As I was on the 15th chew of my 4th bite I looked outside and saw the vendor rep and one of my employees setting out orange pylons about 30 feet apart on one end of the parking lot. Out of the corner of my eye I caught a glimpse of Eric— wearing his Porsche baseball cap—driving his Boxster with the top down in precise Figure 8's while revving up his engine in an obvious attempt to strike fear in the heart of his adversary. I have to admit it was working; I caught myself chewing every bite well more than 23 times as I was trying to figure a way to abort the impending clash of the titans.

'Let's go, Scott.' 'You can do it.' 'Don't let us down.' 'Show him what we're made of.'
My employees were trying to be helpful. Lord, if they only knew.

One of my employees—who drag races at the local speedway on Friday nights in the summer with his hopped-up Camaro and was issued a citation for *drag racing* resulting in a hefty fine, a defensive driving course and an absurd lawyer bill about a year ago—was giving me pointers as I made my way to the other side of the building to get my car. 'Keep the clutch in, rev the engine and then POP the clutch,' he said. 'Yeah, I've had a lot of practice with that,' I thought to myself (I would have said it aloud but my mouth was dry. Go figure.).

I got in my car and noticed another pair of orange pylons with yellow caution tape stretched between them; the official finish line, no doubt. I noticed one of my employees had parked his car long ways across the entrance to our parking lot to keep any vehicles (a police cruiser, for example) from interfering with our festivities.

I drove to the starting line and pulled up next to Eric, my employees urging me to put the top down on my Boxster as well. I complied and, as you might suspect the crowd went wild. The vendor representative asked us to do a trial run to 'get a feel for the track,' all 150 yards of it. Eric and I drove in tandem to the finish line, never getting above 20 miles per hour. We circled back and lined up on the starting line and received instructions from the official starter for the event: Camaro Boy.

'I'll make eye contact with you (looking at me), then with you (looking at Eric), I'll raise my hand and when I drop it you can go.' Simple enough. I glanced over at Eric to see if he was ready and apparently he was: There was now a ski helmet where a baseball cap was the last time I looked.

My employees were about to explode from anticipation, employees from the warehouse next door had gathered as well and almost everyone had cell phones in their hands with the setting on 'video record' as Camaro Boy was about to drop his hand.

It was over in a matter of seconds. I kept my car in first gear for the first 100 yards and opened up a good 15-yard lead on Eric before I eventually shifted into second gear and blew through the yellow caution tape for the win. (That sounded a lot better than it actually was; the shift into second gear was anything but smooth.) We both circled back to the starting line where we were greeted with a loud roar from the crowd, a roar more deserved by the winning team in a Super Bowl.

I was ready to put an end to my drag racing career until the vendor rep called for another race, only this time Eric and I had to 'switch sides' to rule out the possibility that I had won in the 'faster lane.' Less than 30 seconds later I'm happy to report that our second head-to-head matchup ended up the same way as the first; however I'm *not* happy to report that once again I didn't have a very good transition from first gear into second. I know one thing: It felt good hearing an even louder roar on my second triumphant return to the starting line.

After soaking in the accolades for another three or four minutes I drove back to my regular parking space and truth be known I was happier it was over than I was happier I had won (*twice*). Eric followed me in his car and as we shook hands he insisted on a rematch next year. 'Certainly;' I lied. In my head I could hear Apollo Creed: 'There ain't gonna be no rematch.'

I'm happy to say that things couldn't have turned out any better, considering 15 minutes earlier I was chewing every bite of pizza about 75 times and my mouth was as dry as the Sahara: (1) I won. Twice. (2) My employees thought I *rocked*. (3) There was no vehicular damage. (4) I didn't crash and burn (literally, figuratively). (5) The police never knew what we were up to. (6) As far as I know the day's events never made an appearance on either YouTube or Facebook. (7) Have I mentioned I won? As a matter of fact, I did it *twice*.

As I sat in my office basking in victory and contemplating my undefeated career in drag racing I looked out the window and noticed Camaro Boy racing his Camaro back and forth across the parking lot. Apparently he had asked to race against the winner.

Sorry, Camaro Boy: The Legend has retired at the top of his game.

CHAPTER 8

Bet my Sweet A**

———— ⚮ ————

Place a Wager

This year's Super Bowl presented a couple of prospects for doing something I've never done before. Having seen every single one of the first 47 Super Bowls I considered skipping this one altogether, thus making me 'that guy' that didn't see the biggest game of the year….or the newest Dorito commercial. Then again perhaps this would be the perfect opportunity for me to place a legitimate bet for the first time in my life. After all the Denver Broncos, the highest scoring team in the history of professional football was playing a team led by a second-year quarterback. The mighty Broncos were led by Peyton Manning, who this season had passed for the most touchdowns and the most yardage in the history of the National Football league and been named the League's Most Valuable Player for a record fifth time. The line in Las Vegas was Denver by three points: Hell, I would have given Seattle two touchdowns without blinking an eye.

So skip the game, or bet on the Broncos? It seemed pretty obvious to me.

I considered my history of watching the first 47 Super Bowls: The first one in 1967 with my dad in a hotel room in Dallas as we were driving cross-country before moving to Hawaii; the 1969 game and rushing outside at halftime to throw the pigskin in the front yard with my best friend, fighting over which one of us would be Joe Namath; the heart-breaking

1980 game as the Steelers won their fourth Super Bowl in six years by defeating my favorite team, the Los Angeles Rams. (Yes, at one time I actually liked professional football and even had a favorite team—an odd choice in that I had never even been to Los Angeles before.)

Then I considered my tendency to be compulsive about things: Running every day since the fall of 1978 (if I considered the equator as one lap, today I would have been running through Romania—for the sixth time); my quest to run 50 consecutive Peachtree Road Races (this year will make 36); a challenge I met in 2013 by writing a story every single day of the year (published in two books—Parts 1 and 2 of *My Life: Everything But BUY THE BOOK!*). Being only two years away from watching 50 Super Bowls in a row, I deferred to my other option: Placing a sure-fire bet on the Denver Broncos.

The last time I gambled was during college. Cindy and I used to drive from Gainesville to the Ocala Fronton to watch Jai-alai, perhaps the fastest moving sport you may have never heard of. Long story short, it's like a gigantic game of handball played on a three-sided basketball court with the players wearing boomerang-shaped bamboo gloves and throwing a goatskin-covered ball at speeds over 200 miles per hour. The players sported names like Chucho #1, Chucho #2, Javier the third and Ronaldo IV; you know, names you would ordinarily expect to find on a masked professional wrestler from Mexico. We would place $2 wagers on a quinella, meaning we would have to correctly pick the first and second place winners in any order (for example, if we picked Chucho #2 and Ronaldo IV, as long as they were the top two performers we would win the bet, regardless of which one of them actually won the game). We did quite well; if memory serves Cindy and I tended to be a bit compulsive when it came to our Tuesday and Friday night trips to Ocala. The people working at the Fronton may have even considered us as 'regulars.'

So now, 40 years removed from my last real wager, I was faced with finding a bookie. That may have proved difficult, seeing as I've never met a bookie in my entire life. But fortunately I have a friend who has a friend who knows a guy who knows another guy who has a friend who knows a guy who knows a bookie. I gave my friend five $20 bills (the same friend who has a friend who knows a guy who knows another guy who has a friend who knows a guy who can give my money to the bookie), confident I would be getting back *ten* $20 bills after the big game.

A little background before kickoff: The past seven days had been pure hell. Atlanta had a devastating three-inch snowfall (no laughing) the Tuesday before the Super Bowl. My older son totaled his car after hitting a patch of black ice and smashing into a high concrete burb (he wasn't hurt), my younger son had a similar accident and wrecked the front of my prized Gator Truck (he wasn't hurt; I was—emotionally) and Cindy (as well as Justin, since Cindy made an eight-mile four-hour round trip in a snow and ice storm to pick him up on the side of the road) had to spend Tuesday night at her law firm because she couldn't drive home since Atlanta was paralyzed from the snow and ice (like I told you before: no laughing). Then on Super Bowl Sunday our dishwasher decided to call it quits and a couple pieces of tile broke loose from our newly remodeled front porch. Throw in one of our cats 'scooching' across the carpet and leaving behind a couple of brown streaks for me to clean up and I had all the proof I needed that Karma simply hates me.

Once toe met leather and the Super Bowl was officially underway, I had a good feeling about the game's outcome since I was long overdue for Karma to pay me a visit. I should have known better: Seeing my boyhood idol Joe Namath tossing the coin on the 50-yard line before the start of the game wearing a coat made out of polar bear (If I had to guess) should have tipped me off on what was going to happen next. In other words whatever it was, it was sure to be ugly. On the very first snap of the game Peyton Manning was calling signals and took a step towards his offensive line, a split second before the center hiked the ball to the spot Manning had been standing two split seconds earlier. The ball rolled into Denver's end zone for a safety. After 12 seconds of the 48th Super Bowl the score was: Seattle – 2, Denver – 0. The next time Denver had the ball Manning threw an interception. Things went downhill from there: Manning threw an interception that Seattle turned into a field goal. Manning threw an interception that Seattle returned for a touchdown. At halftime the score was 22 – 0. Denver had been hapless on offense for 30 minutes, but things had to improve in the second half; they just had to. Karma, are you listening?

Apparently not. Seattle's Percy Harvin returned the second half kickoff for a touchdown. The play took 12 seconds off the clock, the same amount of time it took Seattle to score in the first half. Ah, so *there's* that Karma I was looking for…

During the week leading up to the Super Bowl the talking heads of the NFL pregame shows were debating about whether or not Peyton Manning should be considered the 'best (quarterback) ever' if he led the Broncos to victory in the Super Bowl. Manning's play on the NFL's biggest stage reminded me of his four years playing quarterback for the Tennessee Volunteers. Against my (*and Percy Harvin's*) alma mater, the University of Florida, Manning's Vols lost all four games by a composite score of 161 – 86, including 31 – 0 and 62 – 37 drubbings in his first two seasons. Ironically, the year after Manning graduated the Vols won the NCAA National Championship led by quarterback Tee Martin, Manning's former backup. Karma can be cruel sometimes.

As the Super Bowl drew to its inevitable conclusion (a 43 – 8 Seattle victory) I was feeling sort of sad I would never have the chance to meet the bookie who knows a guy who has a friend who knows a guy who knows another guy who knows my friend who I gave the $100 to wager for me a few days ago.

As for Karma—well, like I said earlier: Karma hates me.

As for Peyton Manning: He had a sensational season in 2013, broke a lot of records and earned the love and respect of every Bronco fan around the world. But when all is said and done, even though he earns a kazillion dollars a year Peyton Manning and I have one thing in common:

Neither one of us won a Super Bowl this year.

Karma doesn't think much of Peyton Manning either.

CHAPTER 9

Running to Extremes

⟨∞⟩

Experience a Dramatic Temperature Swing

Today is Wednesday, February 12, 2014: The day the Governor of the state of Georgia closed the city of Atlanta.

Let me back up for a moment. Two weeks ago today an unresponsive and unprepared Atlanta became the laughing stock of the nation when three inches of snow resulted in devastation and destruction other cities might experience from an even meaner side of Mother Nature. You know; something along the lines of a tornado, hurricane or earthquake. But then again this is the Deep South, where the ability to drive in the snow is needed about as often as a Georgia native turns down grits at the local Waffle House.

So two days ago, in a public announcement to proclaim a legitimate State of Emergency the Governor—with two-week old egg still all over his face—essentially requested Atlanta to shut 'er down at the prospect of an impending ice storm.

After turning on the television this morning I can only say: Good call, Governor. Your chance of being reelected just improved and maybe, just maybe the late night shows won't use you as fodder in their opening monologues for a while. Then again, the world's busiest airport is closed, the production of Coca-Cola has hit the pause button and perhaps worst of all, the filming of *The Walking Dead* in the Atlanta suburb of Senoia is at a standstill. Let's hope for a quick thaw once the ice storm has run its course.

Speaking of 'run,' today's was rather unique. I left the house this morning around 9:30 and was greeted by a stiff breeze that brought the wind chill down to a brisk 17 degrees. On the streets I encountered numerous broken branches and tree limbs; the last time I had seen anything like it was after a hurricane passed through town. Apparently last night was Arbor Day's evil twin (Pearl Arbor Day?) as the combination of sleet, ice and wind did quite a number on the local foliage, turning the gray asphalt streets into a veritable sea of green. One thing is for sure: Whoever is responsible for cleaning up this mess nature left behind is in for a very busy next couple of days.

But the obstacles on the asphalt were not what made todays run unique: Rather it was the dramatic change in temperature I experienced five miles into it.

As the Governor had advised against driving during the ice storm, and with me being the law-abiding citizen that I am, I followed his advice and opted to run over to the assisting living complex Cindy's dad was living in to take him some personal items he wanted. When I got to his room I opened the door and found him asleep in his bed. I was hoping so much he would be snoring, because a couple nights ago something inspired me to create several colorful analogies to describe snoring. NOTE: I PROMISED MY WIFE I WOULD MAKE IT VERY CLEAR THAT SHE WAS NOT THE SOURCE OF THIS INSPIRATION. *(Are you happy now, sweetheart?)* I *so much* wanted to tell you I found him asleep sounding like his tonsils were caught in a bear trap... or a ballpoint pen being stuck in an electric pencil sharpener... or a dentist cracking open a jaw so he could insert a titanium post to support a crown to replace the incisor on the right side of your mouth since you did such a horrible job taking care of it all these years.

But he was actually sleeping quite peacefully; much more so than Cindy was a couple nights ago. NOTE: THIS IN NO WAY NEGATES MY NOTE IN THE PREVIOUS PARAGRAPH. Which brings me to what made today's run so unique: The thermostat in the room was set at a robust 85 degrees. *(I didn't even know thermostats could be set that high. The thermostat in my car can be set as low as 60 degrees or as high as 80 degrees; anything beyond and the setting reads either 'low' or 'high.')* In other words, the temperature in the room was almost 70 degrees higher than what it was outside. What made matters worse: He woke up while I was in the room and wanted to talk, giving me a good 30 minutes to dry out and get warm before heading back outside for the five miles home.

On the run home it took me a couple of miles before my teeth (and a certain crown where an incisor used to be) stopped chattering and the wet stuff covering my eyeballs (forgive me, for I suck at science) started thawing out. All in all I enjoyed the run, a rather peaceful 10 miles only disturbed by the occasional howl of the wind or the distant murmur of tree limbs being fed into a wood chipper which, if I didn't know any better would have thought was the sound of someone's tonsils being caught in a bear trap.

CHAPTER 10

Biting off more than I can Do

⎯⎯⎯⎯⎯⎯⎯⎯⎯⎯⎯

Run a Marathon when I had No Business Doing So

Before I get ahead of myself, a little background is required.

I ran my first marathon in March of 1979: The Florida Relays Marathon in Gainesville, Florida. A couple of minutes before the race began I asked then Florida track coach Roy Benson for advice for a novice marathoner. Coach Benson's comment eliminated any possibility for misinterpretation: *'Don't run marathons.'*

Fast forward to December 2012: I ran my 200th marathon in Honolulu, Hawaii. The trip to Oahu also served as a 35-year wedding anniversary present for Cindy and I, so having her meet me at the finish line of the marathon was pretty special seeing as she was there to see me start my first marathon almost two generations earlier. (Did she hear Coach Benson's advice? Why yes she did, and thank you for asking.)

There was a period of time when my running partners and I stayed in 'marathon shape' year round, the operative word being 'was.'

Today that is not the case. For the first time in my life as a runner I am not in shape to run a marathon: In between marathons #1 and #200 I've done everything possible to ensure my body is no longer capable of running 26.2

consecutive miles without inflicting a great amount of pain and suffering to a body that probably should have retired to the athletic attic several thousand miles ago.

Getting back to the Honolulu Marathon (# 200, in case you've forgotten): Seconds after crossing the finish line in Kapiolani Park I told Cindy it would be my last marathon. Of course it came with a caveat: *Unless I can get healthy again.*

Last Labor Day I hosted an informal marathon consisting of five 5.2-mile loops. My intent was to run three loops and wait for the other runners to finish so I could get their finishing times and round up the equipment once the event was over. After I finished my third loop I was invited to run a loop with someone I hadn't seen in a while. Before I knew what hit me I had run just shy of 21 miles and spent the better part of an hour catching up with an old friend. Then after I finished my fourth loop I realized I only had a couple of hours left before the last runner would finish so I figured why not make the time go by a little quicker and run one more loop and lo and behold I had accidentally (inadvertently?) run my 201st marathon. *(I speak the truth.)* What made it worse was this: I still did not consider myself to be 'healthy again' thus turning my promise of nine months ago into a lie.

Which brings me to today: I'm on the starting line of the Five Points of Life Marathon in Gainesville, Florida wearing a yellow race number. There is no doubt I should be wearing a blue number just like last year when I ran in the accompanying *half* marathon. But when I signed up four or five months ago I felt certain I would be 'healthy again' by the time the marathon (February 16, 2014) rolled around. My yoga regimen (recommended by a neurosurgeon, no less) seemed to be paying off and I was still maintaining a solid (albeit much slower) mileage base that was very comparable to the distance I was running when I could complete a marathon at the drop of a hat. (Our running group had a slogan back then: *Stay in marathon shape year round because you never know when one is going to break out.* Believe me: I upheld my end of the bargain.) But today I can assure you: In no way, shape or form am I ready to run a marathon: In my entire running career I have never had to make such an admission.

As you may have gathered Cindy gave me a good dose of guilt before I actually made it to the starting line (admittedly I deserved every bit of it). Telling her I would hold off deciding whether or not I would run the full marathon 'until I saw how I felt' didn't seem to do much good, probably because she knows me well enough to know I had no intention (nor the intellect) of opting for the shorter yet-much-more-reasonable distance of the half marathon--regardless of how I felt.

Once the race was underway I stuck to my original game plan of keeping my effort and exertion at less than 100%; I figured it was the only chance I had of gutting out 26.2 miles. As I was running my first mile I noticed the 3:30 marathon pace group pass me by. Soon after the 3:45 marathon pace group did the same. (Note: I should mention that all of the half marathon pace groups passed me by as well during the first mile, even though their race started about 150 yards behind mine.) I reached the first mile marker in a robust 8:51. (I was targeting a nine-minute pace for the entire race, meaning I would be very satisfied with a four-hour marathon.) I was pretty happy with my first mile, at least up until the moment the 4:00 marathon pace group dusted me like there was no tomorrow.

Not the type to be easily dismayed I maintained my pace—give or take a few seconds—for the next 12 miles until I reached the point of no return: The 13-mile mark where a volunteer was stationed to direct the half marathon runners to the right for the last tenth of a mile to the finish line, and the marathon runners to the left for another 13.2 miles of undulating hills and climbing temperatures before they would reach their respective finish line. I turned to the right, only to be stopped by the stalwart volunteer who refused to let me pass seeing as I had a yellow number indicating I had signed up to do the Full Monty and there was no way in hell I would be the cause of him not being named the local running club's Volunteer of the Year in 2014 because he allowed me with a yellow number to run the last tenth of a mile reserved for runners with a blue number. I rehearsed that last sentence in my head so many times over the next 13.2 miles I almost started to believe it myself; I figured I would have no problem selling it to Cindy a couple of hours or so later.

Somehow I managed to maintain the same pace for another 11 miles. I was on pace for a four-hour marathon but was quickly succumbing to the various ailments caused by allowing my 'good' left leg to do most of the heavy lifting for the better part of 24 miles. (More background: My right leg has, for all intents and purposes been on the 'disabled list' since September 2010, which in condensed form explains the yoga, the reduced mileage and the overall non-marathon ready condition I find myself in today.)

But then something inside of me clicked. Maybe it was because I feared this might be my last marathon ever and I wanted to finish it in less than four hours. Maybe it was because I was in Gainesville where I ran my first marathon almost 35 years ago and how cool it would be to run my last marathon—if it in fact turned out to be my last—in the same city. Maybe it was because I wanted to do well in my age group if this ultimately became my marathon swan song and coincidentally there just happened to be two men directly in front of me who *looked* like they might be right around my age.

Whatever it was, I feel comfortable saying I ran those last 2.2 miles about as well as I've ever run 2.2 miles in my life. Was I in extreme pain? Yes. Would I be admitted into an ER if I had run directly into one without breaking stride? Absolutely. Did I FOR ONE MINUTE think I was doing something that could cause irreparable damage to my body in the future? Without a doubt. Did any of this matter? Allow me to clue you in on a little phrase recently introduced in the running community that I've lived by three decades before it ever found its way onto a T-shirt: *Harden the f*** up.* In other words no, none of it mattered at all. The only thing that mattered was running hard enough to finish in less than four hours, regardless of how much it hurt or how much permanent damage it might be doing.

I crossed the finish line in three hours, 55 minutes and 21 seconds. I won my age group. I ran what may turn out to be my final marathon in the city where it all began: Gainesville, Florida. Time to quit while I'm ahead, right? Especially considering Cindy wasn't happy *('But I won my age group, dear!')* that I ran the full marathon and didn't believe my story about the 13-mile volunteer for a second, even though by now I had convinced myself it was the absolute truth.

The next morning I woke up after a restless night with the absolute worst pain in my right kidney: If I didn't know any better I would have sworn it was used as a punching bag by Rocky Balboa because he wasn't able to find a suitable side of beef. As I stumbled into the living room of our good friends Ferit and Gizem Toska-- whom we were staying with for the weekend, I fell onto the couch to watch cartoons with their two-year old son Derin. On the television an animated talking taxi was returning a young boy who had become separated from his mother. As she thanked the taxi for returning her son, the boy took off running to play with his friends. The mother turned and called out to her son:

Don't run, honey. You could hurt yourself.

I think I just might get that phrase printed on a couple of T-shirts. One for me and one for Roy Benson, who told me the same thing almost 35 years ago.

Just not in so many words.

Postscript: It appears I'll be in Gainesville to run the marathon again in 2015—my younger son Josh wants to make it his first and asked if I'd run it with him. Besides, it's the 10th anniversary of the event and Cindy and I will be featured in a local magazine as we're two of the four runners who have run the race every year.

CHAPTER 11

Couch Potato

———— ⨳ ————

Binge Watch an Entire Television Season in One Day

For six years I always looked forward to circling a certain week in August on my calendar; the week Cindy and her girlfriends made their annual pilgrimage to the beach. For that was the week I made my annual pilgrimage to my living room where I would catch up on the latest season of the HBO series *Dexter*. I called the week 'Dexfest' and enjoyed it immensely for the first six years of the show.

However, things changed during seasons seven and eight. Cindy opened her first oil and vinegar store during season seven and her second store during season eight. The girls' pilgrimages to the beach--and Dexfest both came to a screeching halt: To this day I still don't know how things turned out for Dexter Morgan, America's favorite serial killer.

Which is why I was looking forward to this past Saturday: Cindy would be spending the day preparing for a party she was hosting at her store that evening, leaving the entire day for me to do what I wanted to do. Since I had never watched an entire season of any television show in a single day, I thought this presented the opportune time to try binge watching (translation: rendering myself useless for an entire day). I was all set to catch up on season seven of *Dexter* when a friend of mine told me Friday afternoon she was going to watch *House of Cards* over the weekend as she had heard really good things about it. I had heard similar reviews of the show and decided *House of Cards* would be the main course on my Saturday menu.

Doing a little research I discovered season one of *House of Cards* was 675 minutes long, or 11 hours and 15 minutes. Knowing I could fast-forward through the theme song of episodes 2 through 13 (Note: I always listen to the them song during episode 1 of any show just in case it's a really catchy tune—the theme song for Cinemax' *Banshee* being a prime example), that left approximately 11 hours of viewing to squeeze into a typical Saturday. You may be wondering 'How can a Saturday be typical?' I wake up every Saturday at 3:45 a.m. I drink coffee and take care of minor household chores (dirty dishes, laundry, litter box) until 5:15 at which time I drive to Al's house for our weekly 10-mile run. I'm home by 7:35 and take care of errands (grocery shopping, banking business, filling up the gas tank) that normally take me until 10 a.m. Then the rest of the day is mine until I hit the sack around 10 p.m. In other words after my run with Al, I still had enough time to watch 11 hours of television if I didn't stray too far from the living room. The stage was set for the ultimate waste of a day. Here's how things played out.

The day got off to a fast start, as I started watching Kevin Spacey (magnificent in the lead role, by the way) take Washington D.C. by storm while I was having my morning coffee, literally seconds after I woke up. By the time I met up with Al I already had the first episode under my belt. (I might add I was already totally absorbed in the show.)

I went for my every-fourth-Saturday-morning haircut at 8:35 a.m., about 25 minutes before the salon opened. I've known one of the stylists for many years and she always cuts my hair before opening the salon at its official opening time of 9:00 a.m. When I arrived a man and his son were standing outside—in 30-degree temperatures, no less—and the father said to me 'They don't open until 9:00' at the exact moment the front door opened just far enough to let me inside. My haircut took six minutes (as always), leaving another 15 minutes or so before the store was open for business. I volunteered to go out the back door since the father and son were still standing outside, thus sparing my stylist any embarrassing questions when they saw I had gotten a haircut. The stylist took me up on my offer, so I went around the back of the building only to realize I couldn't get in my truck and leave because it was parked about 15 yards from where the father and son were standing and I didn't want them to see I had not only entered the salon 25 minutes before it was open but that I had gotten a haircut as well. So guess who *else* was now standing outside in 30-degree temperature wasting valuable seconds he could be plopped down in front of a television set watching *House of Cards?*

I stopped on the way home to pick up a couple grocery items as well as a bottle of rum Cindy needed for her party, my internal clock ticking all the while as I knew I still only had one episode under my belt. Once I got home I watched the second episode when I decided to take my truck in for an oil change at the garage located about 2 ½ miles from the house. As Cindy was busy preparing for her party I opted to run back home after dropping off my truck, getting home just in time to turn on the television to watch…

The Florida Gators play the Ole Miss Rebels in college basketball. Although they struggled periodically throughout the game the Gators ultimately came out on top. Since the game lasted slightly longer than two hours, I sacrificed watching at least two episodes of *House of Cards* during that window of time but I figured it was worth it: Florida will be ranked # 1 in the country when the next poll is released.

It was now just past 2:00 p.m. and time for me to get down to business. I squeezed in four more episodes before Cindy packed up and left for her store. During this time I only hit the 'pause' button when she was running something through the blender in the kitchen and drowning out the sound of the television. The noise coming from the kitchen was so loud that if I didn't know any better I would have sworn she was making granite milk shakes. I caught a ride to the garage with Cindy so I could pick up my truck and drive it back home: One more errand complete.

It was now 5:30 p.m. and I still had seven more episodes left. It was time to get serious.

As soon as I fed the cats, that is.

Feeding the cats didn't take too much time. However, trying to determine which room one of the cats vomited in afterwards did.

So after finishing cat vomit mop up duty it's now 5:45 p.m. and I still didn't even have my finger on the fast forward button of the remote ready to bypass the theme song of episode seven. *Times-a-wastin'!* It was around 6:30 p.m. when I decided I would also fast forward through the credits at the end of each episode to gain another couple of minutes every hour: Finding out who played the role of 'Hooker # 3' or whom the gaffer (whatever that is) was would have to wait for another day.

From now on it's just you and I, *House of Cards*. For the rest of the evening know this: *Your a** is MINE!*

The final six episodes were easy to digest because they were absolutely *delicious*. Sure, I had to battle back several 90-second naps during the course of the night—the result of a combination of being awake since 3:45 a.m., a busy day of running as well as running errands, lying back in a recliner for five straight hours and two or three (OK, *five*) glasses of Bailey's Irish Cream—but just a few minutes before midnight I was able to claim victory: *I successfully binge watched an entire 13-episode season of a television show in one day.*

Now I figure I can move on to a double-header some weekend in the future: The 7th season of *Dexter* on Saturday and the 8th season on Sunday. It shouldn't that difficult: One season of *Dexter* only consists of 12 episodes, not 13.

Postscript: Later in the year I watched the 7th season of *Dexter*. It took me four days. Someday I hope to watch the 8th and final season, but first there's that little matter of the second season of *House of Cards*...

CHAPTER 12

Sweet Tooth

———————— ✪ ————————

Create a Dessert

I'm always amazed by the number of people I know who are fascinated by The Food Channel. They can name the shows, the stars of the shows and the *soon-to-be*-stars of *future* shows on America's favorite (only?) network catering to (Warning: Cliché dead ahead) the way to a man's heart. My wife is no exception.

Long before Cindy opened her first oil and vinegar store she would stay up late on Sunday nights to watch an elimination cooking competition (think *Survivor* set in a kitchen), the last chef standing rewarded with their own show on which they would one day show the world how to cook the best rutabaga casserole known to man. For the longest time I would tease Cindy because none of the meals she saw created on television in 30 minutes or less ever found its way onto our dining room table.

However that's changed recently. Inspired by the products carried in her store, Cindy has made some of the most amazing meals over the past two years. I have to admit (although I've known it for many, many years): Cindy is one fine cook. She created/invented/whipped up one *incredible* grilled cheese sandwich a couple weeks ago that turned out to be quite a hit at a birthday party her store hosted recently; I am not one bit surprised.

Speaking of surprised, very few people know I do in fact know how to prepare a few dishes of my own. When Cindy and I were dating, lasagna was my specialty. Cindy always enjoyed it, although I'm not sure if it was because she liked how it tasted or because she didn't have to cook dinner that night. Either way my lasagna was always a hit with her. (Chef's secret: If I had to guess I would say that I never cooked lasagna the same way twice. I used recipes printed on the box of spaghetti noodles, on a can of tomato sauce, from an old cookbook and sometimes I would simply rely on trying to remember what ingredients I used the last time. And if I'm ever uncertain if the lasagna may not turn out like it's supposed to, I add a butt load of cheese. I've learned cheese can conceal almost any cooking sin.) I'm also quite adept at putting together a bowl of cereal, cooking a frozen pizza in the oven between 350 and 425 degrees, heating leftover soup in the microwave and pouring a glass of Bailey's Irish Cream over ice (Crushed, cubed, shaved: It doesn't matter; I can do it all). That last one is among my favorites as it always satisfies my sweet tooth. Speaking of sweet tooth…

Once recipe I regret not having is the one my Aunt Minerva (Auntie) followed for making the world's best vanilla cake (my all-time favorite dessert). I used to spend many afternoons in the kitchen with her as she used 'a dash of this' and 'a dash of that.' I often wish I had taken the time to write down all those dashes but Auntie would always talk—and bake as well--really, really fast and it was all I could do to listen, let alone write anything down. Besides, I was only five years old and I didn't know how to write yet anyway.

Time out for an old war story: My absolute favorite baking story that just so happens to be Cindy's absolute least favorite. During college the Betty Crocker recipe cards were popular, and Cindy had quite the collection. One day she tried to bake a cake from a Betty Crocker recipe card for my best friend Stan and I, but for some reason the cake 'fell' while baking in the oven. Once the two layers cooled off, she tried putting one on top of the other and 'patching' the bad spots with the homemade icing. While there wasn't a name for it at the time, there is one now: Epic Fail. Disappointed, Cindy went to the library to study while Stan and I decided to round up the ingredients Betty Crocker called for and gave the cake a shot of our own. Several hours later Cindy returned and found a picture perfect (I cannot imagine a more literal interpretation of the phrase) cake on the dining room table. Standing next to the cake was the Betty Crocker recipe card; the picture of the cake was identical to the freshly baked cake next to it, right down to the tiny piece of parsley positioned in front of the cake plate. (Were Stan and I both in the running for the crown of Ultimate Smartass? Why yes we were, thank you very much.)

So today, following the Florida Gator victory on the basketball court over the Louisiana State Tigers I was inspired to create a dessert recipe of my very own. I don't count the chocolate lover's milkshake I made for Cindy one Valentine's Day that consisted of everything in the grocery store I could find that I considered to be part of the chocolate family: ice cream, milk, candy (everything from Hershey to Godiva), sprinkles and syrup, among other things. (Grocery store managers: Have you ever considered having one aisle designated for all things chocolate? It has potential.) The concoction wound up to be nothing more than a large glass of chocolate sludge, but Cindy pretended to like it anyway so I checked it off in the 'win' column.

Now back to where I was heading earlier: Ladies, gentlemen and Florida Gator fans I give you the recipe for the Victory Vanilla© Milk Shake:

- Several scoops of a premium vanilla ice cream (none of the generic store brand, please; and don't for one second think you can substitute frozen yogurt for ice cream)
- A generous helping of milk (2% or whole only; not skim or 1%-- this is a VICTORY shake, not a LOSER shake)
- A splash of French Vanilla Kahlua (please note: '*French Vanilla*')
- A dash of vanilla flavoring (if you happen to have a bottle of this from Mexico, even better!)
- Equal dashes of Blue and Orange Curacao (remember this is a FLORIDA GATOR Victory Vanilla© Milk Shake and the official school colors must be used; after all, could there be any other reason Orange Curacao even exists?)

Here's where it gets tricky:

- Find a blender.
- Plug the blender into an electrical outlet.
- Put all of the ingredients inside the blender.
- Put the top back on the blender.
- Push any of the buttons on the front of the blender (Note: Not the one on the far left as this would be the 'OFF' button)
- Listen to the sound of the blender until you hear the desired consistency of your milk shake come to fruition.
- Push the 'OFF' button (Note: This should be the first time you touched this particular button. Again, it's the one on the far left. Unless your blender was made in Japan, then it might be the one on the far right but you may have already figured that out two steps earlier.)
- Remove the top of the blender.
- Pour yourself a glass of Victory Vanilla© Milk Shake.
- Enjoy.
- (Repeat if necessary)

As I wash out the blender and stare at the backyard out of my kitchen window, one thought comes to mind:

I wonder what recipe I could come up with using kudzu as the main ingredient?

CHAPTER 13

Bent on Lent

———⊸∞⊸———

Eliminate Diet Soda

I've never truly given up anything for Lent. To do without something that has been a constant in my adult life always frightened me: Hell, if it was in my life it had to be something I either needed or wanted, right? What possible reason could there be for doing without?

According to most of the sources I could find, here is the meaning of Lent:

> *To prepare for Easter by observing a period of*
> *fasting, repentance, moderation*
> *and spiritual discipline.*

OK, point taken: This year I'll give Lent an honest effort. For years my close friends, my distant friends on social media and who could forget, science (damn you, science) have been warning me of the perils of drinking Diet Coca Cola, my beverage of choice. 'Diet Coke can be used to clean the corrosion off of battery cables,' they warned. 'Diet Coke can be used to clean toilets,' they advised. 'Diet Coke can be used to clean the bugs off of the front bumper of a car,' they admonished. OK, OK; as I was saying before, this year I'll give it an honest effort.

The first couple of hours of Day One without Diet Coke weren't too difficult. My normal routine calls for two cups of coffee before my morning run. Hopefully the coffee would provide all the caffeine I needed to make it through the day. For that day—the very first day of Lent—that was the case: The caffeine in the coffee did the trick. However, when I got out of bed the next morning all bets were off. I woke up with a feint headache, blurred vision, a slight touch of vertigo (or perhaps it was nausea; it was hard to distinguish) and a strong urge to go back to sleep. Or die. If I didn't know better I would have sworn I was out late the night before throwing back one boilermaker after another at the Cat's Meow up until when the bartender called for Sven the 285-pound Swedish bouncer to toss me out on my ass because I was creating a scene.

Those first two cups of coffee didn't seem to make a difference. Neither did my run on a windy 40-degree morning that remedied many-a-hangover for me in the '80's. Another mid-morning cup of coffee at the office offered no relief. Neither did the Tootsie Rolls, handful of salted almonds or White Chocolate Macadamia Nut Clif Bar. Maybe a large plate of orange chicken and rice for lunch would do the trick.

Then again, maybe not. The Diet Coke withdrawal pangs continued to go on. And on and on.

And on.

Tick, tick, tick…

Time seemed to pass by slower and slower. Seconds seemed like minutes. Minutes seemed like hours. Hours seemed like days. If Father Time and molasses were in a footrace, molasses would have lapped the old fart too many times to count.

Speaking of 'count:'

Lent lasts for 40 days. Forty loooong days. It's hard to describe the experience, other than to say I can now understand and appreciate what someone with a nicotine addiction experiences when they try to quit smoking or what someone with a running addiction experiences when they try to take a rest day *(don't look at me—I've run every day since November 1978 and if I ever miss a day I swear I'll tear your throat out and did I mention that running is a great stress reliever?)*.

Tick, tick, tick…

Headache. Nausea. Vertigo. Apathy. Anger. Frustration. All caused by the absence of my good friend Diet Coke.

Tick, tick, tick…

My God; when will this end?

Giving up Diet Coke for Lent proved to be one of the hardest things I've ever done in my entire life. And believe me, I know the meaning of pain: I've had a root canal without the benefit of any anesthetic, I've run 135 miles across Death Valley and I sat through an entire performance of *The Nutcracker* in the seventh grade. But giving up Diet Coke? Well, that's just taking pain one step too far.

Forty days? Hell, I barely made it for 40 hours.

But it certainly seemed like 40 days.

CHAPTER 14

An Even Dozen

Run for Twelve Hours

At first glance the idea of running for 12 hours may come across as a bit strange. Perhaps if you knew the reason, it may make it a little less strange. Or quite possibly a lot stranger; it all depends on your perspective.

I've run in races that have required me to run for hours in multiples of six—beginning with six and going all the way up to 36. With one exception: I've never run a race that took me 12 hours to complete.

There were several 40-mile races that took me six hours to complete; my best 100-mile run took me 18 hours (as did dropping out at my first Western States Endurance Run after 62 miles!); there have been several 24-hour timed runs that I stuck around for until the final gun; I finished the Western States Endurance Run (two years after my aforementioned drop) in 30 hours; and I completed a 135-mile jaunt through Death Valley in 36 hours.

Six hours. Eighteen hours. Twenty-four hours. Thirty hours. Thirty-six hours.

I like things neat and orderly. Look in my closet and you'll find shirts of a similar color hanging side-by-side. Look at my compact disc storage unit and you'll find all of them alphabetized by artist. I can always find my car keys, reading glasses and cell phone because I always put them in the same place.

Now you can understand why I needed to run a race that would take me 12 hours to finish: I need my running to be neat and orderly, just like everything else in my life.

With that goal in mind, what could be better than a 12-hour timed run? The Stroll in Central Park 12-Hour Endurance Run in Cumming, Georgia was just what I was looking for. The fact that the Race Director is a friend of mine who always puts on a first class event made the decision even easier. So one cool and breezy March morning I found myself on the starting line—a crack in the asphalt of the 1.03-mile path encircling the baseball and soccer fields of Central Park—ready, willing and hopefully able to keep my feet moving for the next 12 hours.

But before I begin, a little more backstory is necessary.

It's been almost three years since I ran my last ultramarathon (any race longer than the standard marathon distance of 26.2 miles). I swore off running marathons in December 2012 after reaching lifetime marathon #200 (since then I've accidentally run two more, but I digress). Why the long-distance inactivity? One part chronic fatigue, one part old age and two parts various physical ailments that are collaborating to do their absolute best to limit my long runs to no more than 15 miles.

So once I told two people--both well aware of my physical limitations--of my intentions of running for 12 hours, I didn't get a lot of support or encouragement. (My friend Susan was keenly aware of my condition as well; however on this particular day she was also my partner in crime as she was running the 12-hour event with me.) Instead they both made me make a promise they both knew me well enough to know I would have a hard time keeping:

- To my friend Al, I promised I wouldn't run a marathon.

- To my wife Cindy, I promised I would only run 'for a few hours' and 'help out' the rest of the time.

Getting back to the race…

The morning was sensational. At 7:00 a.m. there were the crisp sounds of horsehide meeting metal bats coming from the baseball fields, the enthusiastic screams of supportive parents coming from the soccer fields and the buzz of the runners competing in the 12-hour run all fresh and full of energy, dreams and aspirations of what was to come in the day ahead. I had no complaints the first few hours, as it appeared my physical ailments just might have decided to take the day off.

Around noon I discovered they didn't take the day off; rather, they just slept in late. Once they showed up, the physical ailments made it virtually impossible for me to run each loop without a walk break or two thrown in every 1.03 miles. It wasn't too long after that I had to resort to walking each loop, with a *run* break or two thrown in if I was lucky. In the end it was pretty much all I could do to walk the last couple of loops. It was at this time one of the volunteers posted a picture of me walking on Facebook with the caption: *'Scott Ludwig is NOT running a marathon.'*

It didn't take long for my friend Al to make a comment: *No, but he is probably walking a marathon. Tell him I said to stop. He knows he'll pay for it tomorrow!*

It doesn't take a rocket scientist to know that his final seven words were on the money.

Al hit the nail on the head with his first eight words as well, because I pretty much did walk the equivalent distance of a marathon that afternoon, equating to 25+ long, lonely loops around Central Park.

As for that *first* marathon distance in the morning, however, I *ran* every one of those 25+ loops. So I sort of kept my promise to Al: I didn't run *a* marathon; I actually ran two.

As for Cindy, if it's any consolation, I didn't run the entire duration of the event. Did I run most of it? Yes; but not *all* of it. My 12-hour run will have to wait for another day. So I sort of kept my promise to her as well.

I just love semantics.

Postscript: My 12-hour run didn't have to wait long, as you'll see before you get to the end of this book.

CHAPTER 15

Made to be Broken

Disobey a Law

The following story may or not be based on actual incidents that may or may not have occurred to people that may or may not exist. It could also be a figment of my imagination, a story someone related to me a long time ago or something I dreamed after chasing two dozen oysters with as many bottles of beer that would fit in the silver bucket full of ice the waitress slammed on the table at Big Daddy's a couple of nights ago.

Just know this: Fiction is sometimes stranger than the truth.

Now that I've gotten that out of the way, let's talk law and order. On second thought, law and *dis*order is probably a better way of putting it.

First, a brief history lesson about Johnny Law and I is needed. I've been issued seven speeding tickets in my life: The first was in 1973. I drove off campus (I was a senior in high school at the time) for lunch and on my way back I was pulled over for driving 10 miles over the speed limit (35 MPH in a 25 MPH residential area). My fine was $25, quite a bit to pay for a Huskee Junior and a vanilla shake at the time. My last speeding ticket was in 1985. I was on my way to get a haircut when Power Station's *Some Like it Hot*, my favorite song at the time came on the radio. I drove around the block just so I could listen to the entire song. Big mistake: Once the sounds of the bass came blaring through the speakers my right foot uncontrollably got heavier and heavier, resulting in flashing blue lights and a $75 fine for speeding. In between there were five others, but the sum total of all of my fines is still less than the $750 'super speeder' ticket a buddy of mine received for doing 30 miles over the speed limit on the I-285 perimeter around Atlanta. (If you've never driven on I-285, you should know that driving 30 miles over the speed limit barely keeps up with the regular flow of traffic. Except during rush hour, when you're lucky to be able to drive as fast as 30 miles per hour *under* the speed limit.)

My other encounters with the Men in Blue:

I was involved in an accident—totally my fault as I ran a red light and smashed into another vehicle—and was issued a citation for 'Failure to Yield.' A more suitable citation would have been for 'Flying too Low' or possibly 'DWNBDS' (Driving With No Business Doing So; I trust you can do the math): Believe me: It coulda/woulda/probably shoulda have been a WHOLE lot worse than simply 'failure to yield.'

I was also issued a citation for 'Failure to Move Over.' I won't go into detail—it's been well documented in another book and I don't need to go into any more detail about the incompetency of the judicial system of the sh*thole of a town where it occurred (but if you're interested pick up a copy of *Distance Memories*). Let me just say I doubt I'll ever be sworn in as Mayor of Tyrone, Georgia anytime soon.

Then there was that nasty incident in Albany, Georgia several years ago (also documented in *Distance Memories*—tell the truth: NOW you want a copy, don't you?) where I was the recipient of a failed citizen's arrest. Long story short: Fast marathon + hot day + running shorts drenched in perspiration + not-quite-quick-enough change into dry clothes + public parking lot + local redneck looking for trouble = allegations of indecent exposure.

Now back to the original story.

Sum total: I've been issued nine citations in my lifetime up until now. All were unintentional in the vein that I wasn't *trying* to get a ticket although I will admit to speeding on all seven occasions and (wink wink) failing to yield; I will NOT admit to failing to move over (sorry, but you'll have to read about it in *Distance Memories*).

This made me wonder if I had it in me to *intentionally* get a citation. If I were to knowingly break a law, regulation or rule. After all, aren't rules made to be broken? What's the worst that could happen? A fine? Incarceration? A criminal record? Didn't I have anything better to do with my time? So many questions; it was time to look for some answers.

Before you get all nervous and excited there are two things you need to know:

(1) I am the most law-abiding person you might ever meet. I use my turn signal to turn into my driveway; I live on a cul de sac. If I'm driving I won't take a sip of your incredibly delicious and delightful I-can-almost-taste-it-in-my-mouth home brewed wheat beer if I'm driving—even if your house is a couple of football fields away from mine and we just so happen to live in the same subdivision. So yeah: I follow the rules.

(2) You need to know which 'laws' I wanted to test. There happen to be two obscure laws in Georgia (actually, there are a whole lot more than that. Many more, actually. but I narrowed it down to these two) that I would bet my last dollar a policeman wouldn't recognize if it walked up to him, dropped its pants and pooped on his shoes:

- *No one may carry an ice cream cone in their back pocket if it is Sunday.*

- *It is illegal to say 'Oh Boy' in Jonesboro.*

You can probably imagine in which town I decided to throw all caution to the wind, right? Besides, out of curiosity I wanted to find out if the police were even aware of these two laws. If I was a betting man...

So I headed off to Jonesboro one Saturday morning wearing the loosest pair of pants I could find, knowing I would be putting an ice cream cone in the back pocket at some point. I found a place that sold ice cream cones and sat in the parking lot before realizing the chances of finding a policeman were pretty slim since I hadn't seen one in over 30 minutes and there wasn't a doughnut shop anywhere in sight. I drove to another shopping mall and hit pay dirt: Ice cream cones for sale and a 24-hour doughnut shop right around the corner...with two police cruisers parked right outside. I bought myself an ice cream cone, took a few bites and waited patiently until I saw the two policemen get up from their table inside the doughnut shop and head to the cash register. I carefully slid the cone and its remaining vanilla ice cream inside into my back pocket and headed towards the vicinity of their vehicles in nervous anticipation of getting their attention.

It worked. They both gave me a double take as I walked in front of them. The one with the doughnut powder on his chin elbowed the other (holding a bag of doughnut holes under his arm) and said to me: 'Hey, do you know you have an ice cream cone in your back pocket?'

To which I replied (wait for it...): 'What are you going to do; arrest me?'

(It doesn't get much better than this, people!)

Then this from holder of the doughnut holes: 'Are you being a smart ass, *boy?*'

He had no idea how close I was to having just cause for a citizen's arrest of my own.

But I didn't want to push my luck. After all, they were letting me slide on that ice cream cone caper I was pulling off—whether they knew it or not.

Believe it...or not.

CHAPTER 16

Multi Multi-Task

⎯⎯⎯⎯⎯ ∞ ⎯⎯⎯⎯⎯

Do many, many things at Once

I realized when the year began the majority of the things I would be doing for the first time in my life would be planned in advance. Things like jumping out of an airplane, flame swallowing and wrestling a bear, all of which would require some planning and forethought, not to mention a lot more courage than I'm capable of mustering so forget I even mentioned them.

I also realized some of the things I would be doing for the first time in my life would be spontaneous. Like today, when I was literally doing a dozen things at the same time. Sure, we've all done as many as nine or 10 things at the same time. Think back to the days before you were 'spoken for' and see if this doesn't ring a bell:

Drink to excess, make a fool of yourself on the dance floor, throw up in your bare hands, apologize to your dance partner (if you in fact even *had* a dance partner), desperately look for someplace to set your drink down, make a mad dash to the restroom, stop to pick up the waitress that you accidentally body slammed to the floor, stop to pick up the elderly gentleman you smacked in the face with the restroom door you pushed open with the force of a charging rhino and pull up in front of the urinal literally seconds before you would need to take off your shirt and wrap it around your waist for the rest of the evening thus removing the possibility of embarrassing 'I was there when' stories you would hear from your friends for the rest of your life.

We've all been there, right?

But I bet you've never been where I was today. Then again if you've got a grandson, a cat or two with sensitive stomachs and a non-inflated Spiderman 2 punching bag you may have already done a couple dozen things at the *same time. If you did, it couldn't have possibly played out like this.

> *(*The time span in which these events occurred actually lasted eight, maybe nine minutes.*
> *They were not technically 'at the same time.'*
> *However, as I was 'in the moment' they certainly gave the illusion of being simultaneous.)*

My grandson Krischan and I just returned home from a 90-minute run/walk/oh-look-at-the-ducks! excursion and (1) I tried loading a game on his Leapfrog tablet (a children's version of an iPad, as far as I can tell) using a gift card he got for his 5th birthday two days earlier. It wasn't long before I (2) called Leapfrog's help line, where I was told again and again by a pre-recorded electronic Mary Poppins that my wait to speak to someone would require 'a minimum wait of 10 minutes.'

In other words, allowing me plenty of time to (3) play with Krischan and his new Spiderman 2 punching bag, another of his birthday presents that apparently requires adult intervention. Please note (a) the word 'new,' indicating the punching bag was still in its original 8-inch by 10-inch box and needed to be inflated and (b) there was virtually no difference between the Spiderman 2 punching bag and the original Spiderman punching bag other than the numeral '2' after Spiderman's name. So I removed the non-inflated piece of black and blue rubber from the box and that's when the fun really began...

Because that is when I heard one of the cats tossing her Cat's Meow all over the dining room rug which meant I got to do my absolute favorite (Sarcasm Font) thing in the whole wide world other than being placed on hold on the telephone or inflating rubber punching bags: (4) Clean up cat vomit.

So about the time I got to my knees to start 'picking up the pieces' (if you ever saw regurgitated Cat's Meow you'd understand) I heard Krischan calling out that he 'needs to go to the BAFFroom.' I noticed the urgency in his voice. Seconds later I noticed the urgency all over his shirttail. I asked him to take off 'anything wet' and took the wet garments into the laundry room where (5) I threw everything into the washing machine. As it was a fairly new washing machine, I wasn't familiar with the ringing sound it was making.

Simple explanation: The ringing sound was the front doorbell. So (6) I ran to the door and peered through the glass panels and decided I didn't have any business with two men in their late 20's wearing white shirts and black ties and riding bicycles in 30-degree weather.

Krischan however had other ideas. He walked up behind me, opened the front door and said hello to the two men. Butt nekkid, of course.

However, I (7) seized the opportunity to make myself scarce. I screamed 'Sorry—emergency,' slammed the door in their collective face, grabbed Krischan in all his naked glory and (8) carried him upstairs to put on some dry clothes....

...only to hear the door bell ringing again. And again and again. Aggravated and ready to give the two men at my front door more than they bargained for, I (9) stormed down the stairs, pulled the front door wide open with the rage of the Incredible Hulk etched all over my face and ready to unleash the wrath of the God of Thunder (I love Marvel comics) when the taller of the two men quietly said:

> *'We just wanted you to know your gray cat ran outside*
> *when your son opened the front door.'*

Feeling foolish and to be honest a little bit flattered (see, they thought Krischan was my son) I (10) ran out the front door like the Flash (D.C. comic book reference; sorry to confuse you) and started screaming for Millie (the gray cat), frantically scouring the bushes lining the front of the house.

Meanwhile, a certain naked little boy took the opportunity to grab his box of sidewalk chalk (in a variety of rainbow colors!) to demonstrate his inner Rembrandt all over the driveway, interrupting my search for Millie so I could (11) grab Krischan before the neighbors called the police to report my negligence in the area of adult supervision. I grabbed Krischan with one arm and carried him on my hip as I approached the porch and felt a small bit of relief when I (12) opened the front door with my free hand and saw Millie running hysterically back into the house. 'Gee,' I thought to myself. 'Just what I need: A traumatized cat.'

I noticed the telephone lying on the kitchen counter with the same elevator music playing when I was first put on hold, presumably a lifetime or two ago. A gentle feminine voice was telling me that my 'call was very important' and would be answered as soon as possible.

So while the good people in customer service at Leapfrog were diligently working towards an award for Performance of the Year (please appreciate my special Sarcasm Font), I took the opportunity to (13) dress Krischan and resume Operation Inflation. After blowing into the rubber valve stem and having nothing to show for it, Krischan commented: 'It's not getting *bigger!*' Sadly he was right, which led right into my 'Aha!' moment: (14) 'I'll take the punching back into the garage and inflate it with my electric air pump!' Great concept—the later addition of duct tape around the valve stem and the pump nozzle made it even greater. Before long I was face-to-face with a four-foot tall rubber Spiderman with only one discernable problem: He couldn't stand up straight. (15) Checking the instructions (Instructions for a punching bag? Well of course!) I discovered there was another opening at the bottom that had to be filled 'with sand or water' to ensure Spiderman 2 would stand at attention and return to that position after being punched. (16) I tried adding water by using a plastic cup in the kitchen, and once I got a couple of ounces of water into the punching bag and another couple of pounds of water on the kitchen floor, I had my second 'Aha!' moment: (17) I'll take the punching bag outside and fill the base using the garden hose.' So after (18) connecting the garden hose to the outside faucet, I stuck the end of the hose into Spiderman 2's bottom and filled it with water. OK, I lied because the pressure of the water caused the hose to pop loose from Spidey's butt and I had to (19) reinsert the hose not once but (20) twice until the connection was strong enough to hold.

Once Spiderman 2 was standing tall, I turned around to show Krischan and...*Krischan?* Now where could he be? Where all little boys go to stir up trouble when the last thing you need for them to do is stir up trouble: To visit a nest of red ants in the flowerbed. And by 'visit' I mean 'kick with every fiber of his being.' After (21) brushing off all of the ants I could see on his shoes and pant legs I (22) turned my attention elsewhere: To ME to brush off all of the ants I could see on MY shoes and pant legs. I then (23) kicked off my shoes and (24) removed Krischan's shoes and grabbed his hand and ran inside the house to (25) spray some ointment on our respective red ant bites.

And (26) clean up another splotch of recycled Cat's Meow.

In the background I heard a gentle feminine voice reminding me that my 'call was very important' and would be answered as soon as possible.

Krischan and I went outside where I (27) was going to take out my frustration on Spiderman 2.

I changed my mind when I realized ole Spidey was covered in red ants.

In the distance I could hear the feint sound of a cat disagreeing with its dinner. Again.

I'll stop here, but know this: There was more where this came from. Much, much more.

The Ultimate Runner's High

—⟨∞⟩—

April Fool!

I posted this on my blog, www.scottludwigrunsandwrites.
blogspot.com on April 1.
Not one person realized it wasn't true.

Or WAS it?

Having run every day for over 35 years, I've had the opportunity—or perhaps I should say the misfortune of running in some of the most unimaginable and/or unhospitable places possible. I've run in Death Valley, in the mountains of Sarajevo, on a cruise ship on both the Atlantic and Pacific Oceans and at a rest stop in where-in-hell-am-I, Georgia. I've run on the shoulder of busy highways, in a Wal-Mart parking lot (where I found a bucket worth of loose change), through a cow pasture (paying careful attention not to step on any cow patties) and around the perimeter of a dumpster.

But until today, I've never run at altitude. Not up-in-the-mountains altitude, but honest to goodness up-in-the-air altitude. How does 35,000 feet above sea level sound? Yes, today is the day I can truly say I ran at altitude. Today is the day I ran…inside an airplane.

You're probably wondering: 'In a world of terrorism and TSA agents, how in the world did you get away with running inside an airplane?' I'll just give you the basic ingredients: Proper planning, an international flight at night, good timing and the cloak of darkness.

Here's how I pulled it off:

I booked an evening flight to (European country redacted; my last name may clue you in, however) with an arrival time of 8:00 a.m. That meant I would be flying through the night, a time when most of the passengers would be catching a few Z's. Translation: Fewer eyes observing what was going on in the cabin. Like a strange man running up and down the center aisle for 30 minutes in the middle of the night, for example.

It only took a few hours (the flight lasted eight hours) to determine the ebb and flow of the flight attendants as they worked their way up and down the aisle serving beverages and snacks and pointing out to one particularly annoying man that he was pushing the 'call' button although he kept insisting he was pressing the button to turn on the overhead light. The flight attendants' activity dropped off dramatically around 3:00 a.m. The only movement I could detect was the attractive young couple sitting two rows in front of me across the aisle hightailing it for the lavatory every 75 minutes or so. I felt sorry for them as I couldn't think of anything worse than being held captive on an airplane for over eight hours and having stomach problems requiring the use of the closets they call bathrooms to take care of some nasty personal business. Adding insult to injury: They were on their honeymoon.

Around 3:30 a.m. the coast appeared to be clear: It was time for me to literally make a run for it. I stood up, walked to the front of the aisle, looked around to see if any eyes were on me (there weren't) and slowly took off running for the back of the plane. It didn't take long—maybe eight or nine seconds before I reached the back of the plane. I knew the flight attendants were sitting behind the lavatory, so I was careful to turn around just shy of where I might possibly catch their attention.

I was able to run—unnoticed and undetected for 30 minutes or more. Not pressing my luck, I was satisfied to stop and credit myself with three slow and easy miles at 35,000 feet. What the heck: Let's call it an even 5K (five kilometers, or 3.1 miles).

I wondered if I had been wearing a GPS how it would have recorded my distance—especially if I was running toward the back of the plane. *'If the plane is moving forward at 500 miles per hour and I'm running backwards at six miles per hour, does the GPS recognize this as moving at 494 miles per hour?'* (In hindsight I'm sorry I mentioned it. If thinking about this keeps you up at night, I apologize.)

About the time the pilot announced it was time to prepare for landing, a flight attendant leaned over my seat and pinned a pair of wings—the kind they give to small children the first time they fly on an airplane—on my collar. She looked at me, smiled and said I gave new meaning to the phrase 'Mile High Club.' Apparently she had seen me earlier as I was wearing out the carpet of the center aisle while everyone else on the plane was asleep.

Well, *almost* everyone.

As I stood up to exit the plane I noticed a pair of wings just like mine on the collars of both of the newlyweds when it suddenly dawned on me:

They weren't having stomach problems. They were becoming members of the Mile High Club the old fashioned way.

From what I saw of them throughout the night, it might be more appropriate to recognize them as 'frequent flyers...'

CHAPTER 17

That Little Boy Smell

———— ❧ ————

Be Young Again (if only for one day)

Everyone knows the smell. Anyone who has ever been around a small, energetic boy, that is.

The slight odor of dried perspiration, the feint hint of stale puppy dog breath and a sprinkle or two of good ole' dirt and grime for good measure. Yes, that would be the smell of a little boy after a full day of—well, being a little boy.

One generation removed from having two little boys of my own, I am now the proud G-Pa of an energetic, never-sit-or-stand-still grandson. Today we were going to do things little boys enjoy doing. Or as he told his Yia-Yia (grandmother) before she left for work: 'Today we're doing *man* things.'

First thing on the agenda: Hanging a wind ornament in the yard, a Christmas present I received last year from Yia-Yia. (It might have been three years ago, perhaps as many as five.) If I do say so myself: We did a great job and the ornament looks fantastic. It made me wonder what took me so long. It also made me wonder how much longer it would have taken had Krischan not insisted we hang it *today*.

Next came a trip to the store to buy some much-needed accessories for the day: Ice cream, a Tee-ball baseball glove, a collage-style picture frame, a two-pack of Teenage Mutant Ninja Turtle toothbrushes (one for G-Pa and Yia-Yia's house and one for Daddy's house) and enough boxes of Hot Tamales (or 'spicy candy,' as Krischan calls it) to keep our tongues in red dye for the rest of his three-week visit with us.

What would a trip to the store be without a stop at the Golden Arches* on the way home? (*A clever ploy on Krischan's part to make his way to McDonald's indoor playground, one of his favorite respites. I fell for it. Again.)

Once we got back home it was time to 'break in the leather.' But first things first: I had to explain how a right-handed boy should wear a baseball glove on his *left* hand; not nearly as simple as it sounds. Granted, Krischan may in time prove to be ambidextrous (he is equally adept at throwing things hard with both his right and his left hand) but for the sake of today's lesson I assumed he'll eventually be a pure righty. He managed with the glove for a while, up until the point his 'hand got sweaty' and he switched the glove over to his right hand. From that point on he was catching the ball in the web of the glove on his right hand (good) but trying to throw the ball back to me Jai-Alai style with the ball still in his gloved right hand (bad).

Now it was time for some 'man things,' meaning things I have done for many years but if I had my druthers someone else would be doing them. Like pulling weeds in the garden along the side of our yard. Or in this case, getting rid of the 'snake creatures' that were trying to infiltrate the garden along the side of our yard. Is there a better 'snake creature catcher' than a grandson? I think not! (Score one for G-Pa.)

Is there a better reward for a job well done for a five-year old boy than handing him a box of sidewalk chalk and telling him to go crazy on your driveway? If there is I'd like to know about it, because Krischan's face lit up like mine had 30 minutes earlier when I saw Krischan catch a ball in the web of his glove (at the time on the correct *left* hand) for the very first time in his life.

We took a break from the brilliant springtime afternoon sun and went inside to rummage through countless family photos until we found the perfect six—three horizontally framed and three vertically framed—to fit into the photo collage frame. It would be a gift for Papa, Krischan's great grandfather later in the day.

But before that, Krischan and I went for our afternoon run (and walk whenever Krischan's 'heart hurt'). We ran (and walked) by the usual spots: The lake on the 18th hole of the Braelinn Golf Course that is inhabited by a baby-duck-eating shark; the tunnel running beneath Braelinn Road 'where the Ninja Turtles live;' and the tool shed on the 2nd hole of the golf course 'where zombies sleep.' That grandson of mine has quite the imagination: That shark couldn't possibly discriminate between baby ducks and adult ducks, and did he even consider adolescent ducks? Seriously, sometimes that boy just doesn't think things through.

Our final stop of the day was the assisted living complex where Papa has been a resident for the past four months. Seeing Krischan brought a *huge* smile to Papa's face. As the three of us made our way out to the commons for a walk around the grounds I noticed Krischan had a similar affect on the entire Memory Care Unit, residents and staff alike. An effervescent five-year old boy and his infectious smile will do that to a person. After our walk we sat outside and enjoyed the bright sunshine and the cool afternoon breeze. I managed to snap a couple of photos of the two of them—separated in life by 83 years but today as close as a great-grandfather and great-grandson could possibly be. We escorted Papa to the dining hall for his dinner, me holding one arm and his great-grandson ever-so-carefully holding onto the other. Krischan only let go of his death-grip to run ahead and hold open any doors in our path.

When we returned home it was time for a bath. Krischan wanted to 'wash the sweat out of his hair' after a full day of being a boy.

After a day like today there is no doubt in my mind he had that little boy smell.

But you can't take my word for it. I couldn't tell.

Most likely because I smelled like a little boy, too.

CHAPTER 18

Cuckoo for Coconut

———— ⚭ ————

Eat Coconut

I have never had a particular affinity for coconut. I guess a lot of that has to do with the fact that coconut has no discernable taste. In fact the only thing coconut has is a distinct texture.

Case in point: When I was a student at the University of Florida I was a waiter at my fraternity house. That meant two things: (1) I ate dinner before the brothers and pledges every night and (2) I had unlimited access to anything on the menu before it reached the dining room tables.

So one evening I conducted a test to prove my theory that coconut lacks any distinguishing taste. The dessert on that particular night was coconut cake, which is nothing more than vanilla cake topped with vanilla frosting sprinkled with coconut shavings. Unbeknownst to everyone I substituted the shredded coconut with about 20 yards of dental floss (the waxed kind) I had cut into small ¼-inch strips. I don't have to tell you how many brothers or pledges noticed my switcheroo but I can tell you it was somewhere between none and none.

OK, I may have misled you earlier about my feelings for coconut. I actually *hate* the taste of coconut. The exception, of course would be the coconut cream used in the creation of a Pina Colada. I developed a fondness for

Pina Coladas and other similar frou-frou drinks in my 'Happy Hour Days' of the early-to-mid '80's: Amaretto Sours, Grasshoppers and White Russians immediately come to mind. Of course those days are long gone, but it's kind of reassuring to know that if I were to lose all my teeth and am forced to convert to a liquid diet I could survive with frou-frou drinks as one of my four major food groups.

Granted, coconuts have been portrayed rather glamorously on television for many years. The seven castaways of the SS Minnow survived on little more than coconuts for three years in the mid-'60's. Coconuts (along with white rice) have been the go-to source of nourishment for the cast of *Survivor* for more than a decade. But try as I might, I just couldn't get past the thought of knowingly or willingly putting food with no taste inside of my mouth.

But that all changed a couple of days ago when a friend of the family showed up at our house bearing a gift: A yellow coconut cake from McClure's Bakery in Gap, Pennsylvania. The cake was made from an old Amish recipe and when the top of the cake plate was removed the sweet aroma immediately filled the room and transported me back to my Aunt Minerva's kitchen over a half-decade ago as she leaned over to take one of her magnificent homemade vanilla cakes out of the oven (see Number 12 – Create a Dessert).

As you might imagine, I simply HAD to have a bite of that cake to see if it could possibly—someway, somehow resemble the cake I hadn't had for over 50 years. What was I to do?!? Well, for starters I spent a good 15 minutes or so with a magnifying glass and a pair of tweezers trying my best to remove the white shreds of death littering an otherwise perfect creation. While I didn't get every last piece of coconut, I did manage to extract a composite 15 inches or so.

So with Gilligan whispering encouragement in my left ear and Jeff Probst in my right, I decided to give coconut a try and take a bite.

And what a first bite it was! JUST LIKE AUNT MINERVA'S! The aroma wasn't a tease; *it was the real deal!* Before I knew it our family friend, my son

Josh and I took a lot more bites and before we knew what hit us devoured about 45% of the cake. The family friend accounted for about 5%, Josh maybe 15% and I imagine I was responsible for the remaining 25%. The next night the family friend took us out for brick oven pizza, one of my favorites and I stopped two pieces shy of finishing a personal pan pizza so I would have room in my stomach for another piece or two of the cake when we returned from the restaurant. The third day—the cake's last day on earth—I ate what was left on the cake plate. When all was said and done I had probably consumed the better part of an entire coconut over the course of those three days, not to mention essentially an entire cake as well.

I ate coconut willingly and without incident. I won't do it again: I'm not pressing my luck.

The next time I run across a coconut cake, it might just possibly be laced with shreds of dental floss (the waxed kind).

By the way, I lied earlier: I didn't really cut 20 yards of dental floss into ¼-inch strips during college. I was much too lazy for that back then.

I actually cut the dental floss into 3/8-inch strips.

CHAPTER 19

Yes Man

———⚬⚬⚬———

Learn from a Five-year Old

After spending a lot of time the past three weeks with my grandson Krischan, I've become pretty familiar with his level of proficiency with the English language. I have to admit: For a barely five-year old boy, he's got quite the way with words. I especially like his go-to response on the rare occasion when I had to admonish him with an ever-so-slight reprimand: *'You hurt my heart.'* This, of course is then followed up with slouched shoulders and lips extending all the way down to his chin. It was all I could do to keep from chuckling out loud or at the very least giving him a great big G-Pa hug.

One word that appears to have disappeared from Krischan's vocabulary is the word 'no.' In fact the only time I recall Krischan using it was after he jumped in the tub for a bath and I told him I wanted to wash his hair so he could relax and enjoy playing with his rubber dolphins (a mother and her three calves) until his toes started turning into prunes. If it wasn't for the fact that the shampoo (a) was tear-free, (b) smelled like watermelon and (c) featured SpongeBob SquarePants on the bottle, I probably wouldn't have stood a chance. Thank goodness for American marketing.

The word—other than 'G-Pa, of course—that I heard most often was simply: 'Yes.'

No matter what the question, the answer was always the same.

'Do you want to go for a really long run that will make us super tired?'

'Do you want to try a bite of this? It's really, really hot.'

'Do you want to go for a ride in the car with the top down even though it might rain and we'll get wet?'

'Do you want to throw a penny in the fountain and make a wish?'

'Do you want me to read a scary book to you?'

'Do you want to play catch? Throw the football? Shoot baskets?'

'Do you want to dig for worms? Look for ants? Chase the squirrels?'

"Do you want to take a walk in the woods and look inside the old shack where zombies probably live?'

'Do you want to get on a rocket ship and fly to the moon?'

The answer was always the same: 'Yes.'

The kid is one part adventurer, one part thrill-seeker and three parts fearless. And without a doubt, the kid is…100% boy.

Several nights while Krischan was with us I was a bit surprised by something he said 'yes' to, seeing as 'no' was the answer I had been getting for the first five years of his life. After a rather full day of (as we called them) 'man things' I asked him just after 9 p.m. if he was ready to put on his Ninja Turtle jammies and go to sleep. You can imagine my surprise hearing the word 'yes' where the word 'no' used to live.

I learned a lot these past three weeks. I learned life can be more exciting when you're willing to take risks. I learned life is a lot more fun when you're willing to try new things. I learned life is a lot more—*exhilarating* when you're willing put your fears aside and just go for it. No matter your age, there's a lot to be learned from an inquisitive, wide-eyed and willing-to-give-everything-and-anything-a-chance five-year old boy.

With 30 more new things to try during the remainder of 2014, these past three weeks have put things into a different perspective. I'm going to have to be more adventurous, thrill-seeking and downright fearless if I'm going to make this year different....make this year worthwhile.

At 59 years of age, I've still got new things to learn.

I've still got new things to do.

Most of all, I've still got new things to *live*.

If you have any doubts, just ask Krischan.

Sleeping and Driving Don't Mix

———— ⬦⬦⬦ ————

Sober Up

I was reading this week's issue of *Sports Illustrated* (April 21, 2014) and saw where some talking head said 'athletes should sleep about 8.2 to 8.4 hours per 24.' Then this little nugget: 'A person who goes a week with four hours of sleep per night has impairment equivalent to a blood-alcohol level of .1%.'

So immediately my thought balloon kicked into hyper drive:

*Is a person who has run 10 miles a day for over
35 years considered an 'athlete?'*

*If so, what if this athlete averaged 5 ½ hours
of sleep 'per 24' for those 35+ years?*

*Wouldn't that translate to at least a blood-alcohol
level of .08, the legal limit in Georgia?*

Has this person in fact been 'legally intoxicated' for well over three decades?

If the last question can be answered with a simple 'yes' it would explain a lot. It might very well be the reason:

- Sometimes I can't remember if I ran a particular ½-mile loop through a particular subdivision during my morning run. Fortunately I can usually tell by looking at my chronograph once the run is over. Well, except for the morning runs when I have to make a pit stop (or two) at the 24-hour Kroger because those intermittent times out always mess up my splits.

- I can't find the former Yugoslavia on a world map, even though I went on a ski trip to Sarajevo in 1985—the year after the Winter Olympics were held there. Truth be known, I'm not sure I knew where Yugoslavia could be found on a world map even when it was still known as Yugoslavia. Then again, geography has never been one of my strong suits.

- I have a tendency to bounce off objects (walls, desks, automobiles) to the left of me. Then again, balance has never been one of my strong suits, either.

- I watched the 4ᵗʰ *Die Hard* movie a couple weeks ago and couldn't remember if I had seen it before. To make matters worse, after I watched it all the way through I still didn't know.

- I spent 10 minutes looking around the house for one of my shoes, only to realize one shoe was in my hand and the other on my foot. (Note: More than once. Much more.)

- If it weren't for GPS I would never find anything, regardless of how clear the directions are, how prominent the signs are leading to the destination or how familiar I am with the route because I drive it at least once a week.

- Bad hair days? I have bad balance days, bad coordination days, bad articulation days, bad vision days and bad (Read: incredibly short) attention span days. Not to mention the Good-Lord-why-am-I-having-so-much-trouble-eating-corn-on-the-cob days (1/3 or it all over my mouth, 1/3 of it in my mouth and the other 1/3 on my shirt).

- I occasionally can't remember if I brushed my teeth in the morning. The easiest way for me to know is to squeeze the bristles on my toothbrush to see if they're still wet. If so, then I check the bedroom to make sure none of the cats are under the bed, thus ruling out the possibility that said cat(s) chewed on my toothbrush while I was in the shower.

- *Possum Kingdom* by the Toadies (1995) was playing during a music trivia competition one night and for the life of me I couldn't remember the name of the song. That song has now been around for almost 20 years and I imagine I've heard it a couple hundred times and have known the name of it every single time, except for the one time when it really mattered.

- I tend to trip over things I've never tripped over before. Slight cracks in the sidewalk, small cat toys, sticks with diameters larger than a plastic straw, plastic straws…

- I hit a personal low when I couldn't remember if Rhode Island was a state. To make matters worse I once lived in Quonset Point for three years. You know: As in Quonset Point, Rhode Island.

So I'm feeling a little bit better about myself. I've firmly established that I have IN FACT been legally intoxicated almost every single day since the early '80's. Excluding, of course the two or three days each year I manage to 'sleep in' that never amounts to anything more than seven hours of sleep. In other words, when I sleep in it's the equivalent of starting the day with only a couple shots of Peppermint Schnapps instead of my usual six-pack of beer.

As far as the immediate future is concerned, the talking head in *Sports Illustrated* went on to say 'if you only sleep five to six hours per night *(Guilty!)* a two to three hour-snooze in the afternoon could be your savior.'

Say no more, talking head: I'm buying what you're selling. I love naps.

Let's just hope my boss and wife feel the same way.

CHAPTER 21

Easter Service

———— ⧜ ————

Plan Easter for an Adult

First things first: This idea was entirely that of my wife. I was just along for the ride.

After decades of focusing Easter Sunday around our sons and later our grandson—coloring and hiding Easter eggs, attending Easter service at church and a family dinner at the end of the day—this year Cindy planned the holiday with her dad as the primary focus. On paper and definitely in theory her plan was simple: The two of us would go to church, volunteer at the information counter after the service and have brunch with her dad at the assisted living center where he is living. It looks pretty easy on paper, doesn't it? In theory, even easier.

However, Cindy left out one little detail. Reality. And sometimes—as the movie of the same name will tell you—reality bites.

So here goes, from the top:

I wake up at 4:20 a.m. as I do every Sunday. The plan was to run 14 miles with Susan. However I received a text from Susan she sent somewhere in the neighborhood of 3 a.m. after returning from the veterinary center in Auburn, Alabama where she had to take one of her foster dogs who had fallen ill. She wouldn't be running with me, so I was left to do the 14 miles alone. Running solo was probably the best thing that could have happened to either Susan or me since I had to stop no less than three times during those 14 miles to 'take care of business.' I'm not sure why Susan had to take her foster dog to the clinic, but I imagine if I had four legs and a tail I would probably be on my way to Auburn as well.

I recovered in time to make the 10:30 service at church. As he is prone to do on Easter Sunday, the pastor spoke a little longer than usual during his weekly message. I've noticed that the length of his message is directly proportional to the importance of the day it is given. Easter apparently has earned the top spot on the pastor's list. As Cindy and I worked the information counter afterward, the only question posed to me was by a woman who asked how many seats there were in the church. I told her I would guess around 600 and asked her if she had a minute for me to go and count, but apparently she had to take her pet to Auburn because she left in a hurry without saying goodbye. However, curiosity got the better of me and I went to count the seats and I bumped into the pastor. Instead of telling him I enjoyed his special Easter message he delivered 10 minutes earlier, I asked him how many seats there were in the church. 'A little over 500,' he replied. Thinking to myself that my guess of 600 wasn't too shabby, I had no idea at that time it would be the high point of my day: Brunch was right around the corner and as the beginning of my day was trying to tell me, karma was most definitely *not* on the menu.

(A word about Lee, Cindy's dad. He is 88 years old. He suffered a brain aneurysm over 20 years ago. He experiences bouts of dementia. He misses his home in Jacksonville, Florida where he lived with his recently deceased wife Eva for 67 years. He has been living in a room in the memory care unit at a nearby assisted living facility for the past five months. He doesn't drive anymore, although he does have a valid Florida driver's license. He wants nothing more than to return to Jacksonville, buy a 'two bedroom luxury condo,' find a small car he can drive in comfort and let his friends and neighbors care for him until he is reunited with Eva. The truth of the matter is: None of that will ever happen with the exception of the reunion with his wife. Everyone knows it. Everyone, that is, except Lee.)

Cindy and I found Lee in his room in a long-sleeved dress shirt, a pair of white canvas slacks and his black Bostonian dress shoes. More importantly he was wide awake and instantly hit us with his desire to return to Jacksonville as soon as we were able to get some time off from work to take him. Cindy reminded him it was Easter Sunday and time for all of us to be together as a family; we could talk about Jacksonville later.

So off to the dining area we went. June, one of the residents of the memory care unit was already seated. Lee, Cindy and I filled the remaining three seats, rounding out our party of four. There was a plate of roast beef and vegetables next to a bowl of salad and a glass of tea in front of Lee. Cindy and I were free to hit the buffet table...around the corner, through the door and down the hall where the other residents were dining.

Lee: 'I'm not hungry. If I eat anything I will VOMIT! When can I get to Jacksonville, Florida, Cindy?'

Cindy: 'Lee, remember this is EASTER. It's a time for us to be together. Let's not talk about Jacksonville today.'

Lee: 'OK. I'll honor your request. But I want to go back to JACKSONVILLE, FLORIDA. The SOONER the BETTER.'

Cindy looks at me, silently mouthing the words 'help...me.'

June: 'Eat your food, Mr. Martin. It's going to get COLD!'

Lee: 'I'm not hungry. If I eat that food I will VOMIT! You don't want me to VOMIT, do you?'

June (looking at me and rolling her eyes): 'That man never shuts up.'

(For the sake of argument please pretend I'm just a fly on the wall taking notes. I try to refrain from conversation with Lee in a public setting because (a) he talks loud enough for anyone within 100 yards to hear and (b) if you didn't already figure it out, he's extremely hard

of hearing—especially without his hearing aid he accidentally stepped on a couple days ago and broke in half. So again: I'm not here.)

Cindy: 'Are you not going to eat, Lee? The roast beef looks delicious.'

Lee: 'I WANT TO GO BACK TO JACKSONVILLE, FLORIDA. I want to make my OWN DECISIONS. This place you put me in is FINE, but I want to go back to Florida and get my finances in order.'

Cindy: 'It's Easter, Lee. A time for us to be together…with you.'

June: 'Eat your food! It's getting cold.'

Lee (looking angrily at June): 'You don't tell me what to do, missy.'

(About this time another resident of the memory care unit is seated at the table next to us. He is seated with his back to us. For a reason, I soon found out. I'll call him 'Mr. X.')

Mr. X (loudly and to no one in particular): 'My nose is running like a faucet.'

Lee: 'I want to go to Jacksonville. When can I go to Jacksonville? I used to sell frozen food in Jacksonville, Florida. I went all the way to Iceland to find fish for Burger King. *(This is an abbreviated version of—as I call it—'the Iceland caper.' Other stories that may or may not have been told on this particular day include 'the Utah incident,' 'Cindy's peck on the cheek,' and 'the bonus.' Some day when I have more time…)*

June: 'Mr. Martin, will you please just SHUT UP?'

Lee: 'When can we go to Jacksonville, Cindy?'

Mr. X (louder than the first time and again, to no one in particular): 'My nose is running like a faucet.'

Lee: 'Can we go to Jacksonville TODAY?'

Cindy: It's Easter, Lee.

As I mentioned earlier, reality bites. So does the Easter Bunny, apparently.

Postscript: Lee enjoyed a rather peaceful and thankfully uneventful Thanksgiving and Christmas dinner with Cindy and I. In the privacy of our own home, of course. After all, we weren't born yesterday.

CHAPTER 22

Get High

Overcome my Fear of Heights

After thorough investigative research, I have found the 10 most common fears are (in ascending order):

10. Fear of commitment (commitmentphobia)
9. Fear of spiders (arachnophobia) and/or snakes (ophidiophobia)
8. Fear of rejection
7. Fear of failure (kakorrhaphiophobia)
6. Fear of dying (thanatophobia)
5. Fear of intimacy
4. Fear of the dark (nyctophobia)
3. Fear of heights (acrophobia)
2. Fear of public speaking (glossophobia)
1. Fear of flying (aviophobia)

I learned two things from looking over this list (also in ascending order):

2. Apparently I'm not very 'common,' as I only have one of these 10 most 'common' fears.

1. The one common fear I have is not my fault; it's hereditary.

Let me expound on the nine I don't have:

10. I married my high school sweetheart in June of 1977. We remain married to this day. I've run every day since November 30, 1978. Color me committed (it's a reddish brown; you might even call it 'auburn').

9. I had a pet boa constrictor my freshman year in college. I never knew if it was male or female but it didn't really matter, seeing as I named it 'Alice' after my favorite rock band at the time, Alice Cooper.

8. I played one season of Little League Baseball, one season of middle school football and one season of junior varsity basketball. There was a reason I decided to quit after one season of each. Besides the fact I made three coaches very, very happy with my decisions, I discovered rejection to be the least of my fears.

7. I tried running 100 miles through the Sierra Nevada mountain range in 2004 with virtually no trail-running experience to my name. I tried running 135 miles through Death Valley in the middle of July in 2003 without ever setting foot there. I asked Dolores Ruiz, the best-looking girl in Moanalua Intermediate School to go steady with me the first time I ever talked to her. Any questions?

6. Thankfully the jury is still out on this one. But I do realize that every day I'm one day closer to finding out and now that I put that thought in writing it's going to stick in my mind for—hopefully—another 30 years or so.

5. All of my close, long-time running friends know everything there is to know about me, inside and out. I can say the same thing about them. Ask any long-distance runners if they have a fear of intimacy and they'll tell you the same thing.

4. I love the dark. I'm either sleeping or running when it's dark, two of my favorite things in the whole wide world. Once in a while I can do both at the same time. Ask any long-distance runner if they can sleep and run at the same time and they'll tell you the same thing.

2. There is nothing I like more than to get up in front of several hundred people and talk...as long as the material is (a) light in nature, (b) about running or other topics I enjoy and/or (c) supported by audio/visual aids. I've been fortunate to speak to hundreds of people under those conditions on several occasions. Do you know what would have made those speaking engagements even better? If I were (d) paid for them.

1. The simple fact I flew a total of 40 hours round-trip to South Africa and back is all the evidence I need to prove I don't have a fear of flying. The simple fact I will never fly 40 hours round-trip to South Africa ever again is all the evidence I need to prove I have a modicum of common sense. The simple fact I used the word 'modicum' in a sentence is all the evidence I need to prove I don't care if any University of Georgia graduates know what I'm talking about.

Now, about that one remaining thing *I do* have a fear of...the one that causes me to uncontrollably break out in a cold sweat...my pulse to double in the blink of an eye...my a** to (Editors note: This passage was deemed unsuitable for the PG13 rating the author was targeting, therefore it was removed.)... Yes, *THAT* one...the one I skipped over in the list above.

Number 3: Fear of heights.

The first time I noticed I was predisposed to acrophobia was when I was nine years old. We were on a family vacation in France and had the opportunity to visit the Eiffel Tower. We had the option of climbing the stairs all the way to the top, but my dad was satisfied with stopping on the first level; that was as far as he was willing to go. I had mixed feelings at the time, as I was disappointed we didn't make it to the top yet at the same time relieved that was as high as we were going. I couldn't explain those mixed feelings at the time, but several years later when we visited the Empire State Building and my dad refused to go to the top, I was totally on board. I realized then and there: Heights creep me out.

I've run the Jacksonville River Run several times. The course crosses the St. John's River twice: Early in the race over the Main Street Bridge and then again late in the race over the Isaiah Hart Bridge. The Main Street Bridge isn't particularly high, but most of it is grated so if you are looking down you can see the water of the St. John's beneath your feet. You would be right in assuming I ran that section of the race pretty hard. The Isaiah Hart Bridge, however is high. Extremely high, in fact. So high that there is always a strong breeze, regardless of what might be happening at sea level…way down below. The majority of the runners will stay close to the guardrail at the edge of the bridge, the shortest possible route and therefore the wisest route to run if you're looking to run the tangents. I, however always chose to stick close to the large cement median in the center of the bridge. I didn't want to take any chances of a sudden gust of wind blowing me over the guardrail at the edge of the bridge if I absent-mindedly decided to run the tangents. I also didn't want to look down. It's hard to believe this was the same person who asked Dolores Ruiz to go steady in the sixth grade…

So today at work I decided to see if I could summon the strength to try out for the JV basketball team in the dark with a snake in my pocket.

I asked Tim, one of the employees at my warehouse to take me up in a cherry picker (it's like a forklift, except the operator elevates *with* the forks as it extends upward). I put the safety harness on and in the blink of an eye we were a couple feet away from the 32-foot ceiling. I didn't bat an eye, my pulse didn't quicken and I could actually look straight down without wetting my pants. Everything was fine… until Tim decided it would be fun if he 'rocked' the platform we were standing on from side to side. That's when heredity kicked in.

The chances of a 136-pound man rocking a two-ton cherry picker side-to-side and causing it to tip over were about the same as me winning the lottery when it reaches the $500 million mark. But today was the day my life would be changing: I'd pack up and leave and move to the Swiss Alps and live the rest of my days in my $20 million dollar mountain home overlooking the most luxurious ski resort in Switzerland. In other words, today would be the day the cherry picker would be tumblin' down.

Once I managed to summon enough saliva to articulate 'take me down *now*'—and then got my feet back on the ground, I put a spider in my other pocket and decided to board a plane for South Africa.

'Isn't there a hatch that leads to the warehouse roof?'

Tim led me to a mezzanine in the middle of the warehouse and asked me to follow him up the perfectly vertical ladder—all 10 rungs of it—to the hatch allowing access to the roof. I noticed the top of the hatch was about four feet higher than the last rung of the ladder, so a lot more physical effort was required to get to the roof than I thought. Or psychologically planned for, either.

'What if I can't get my 59-year old body over the top of the hatch, slip and fall straight down?' As far as I was concerned, the Isaiah Hart Bridge seemed like small potatoes compared to what I was now facing.

With a death grip on the sides of the hatch I pulled myself over and onto the roof. Tim was already standing by the ledge, looking straight down and encouraging me to come and take a look. Tim wasn't aware how large the spider in my pocket had grown or that I was now in my 30th hour of flying on an airplane.

'This is as close as I get.' I was at least 10 feet away from the ledge. My feet had a death grip (if that's even possible) on the roof. I recalled the time I went to the top of the Sears Tower with a group of friends. I exited the elevator that runs directly up the center of the building when we reached the top floor, only to realize I was surrounded by glass. You could see Chicago in every direction. I stood with my back against the enclosure

around the elevator shaft with my palms glued to the wall; a reverse-spread eagle, so to speak. I never took *one single step* towards the glass. In any direction.

So instead Tim walks over to me. The b*st*rd starts jumping on the roof. I notice the roof is bouncing as he jumps. I immediately begin assessing the situation: If a 136-pound object repeatedly strikes a load-bearing roof from a height of six inches, at what point does the roof become compromised?

I head for the hatch, dreading the four-foot drop to the top rung of the ladder. I slither like a boa constrictor over the top of the hatch until my left foot strikes pay dirt. Now if I can just...get...my...right...foot...

I've done it! Just nine more steps and I'll be *home free!*

Nine slow, agonizing, meticulously taken steps later I'm back on terra firma (loosely translated from Latin to mean *'Thank you sweet Jesus'*). Safe and sound, although now I'm wearing a shirt almost completely drenched in perspiration from a fear-induced and panic-stricken cold sweat. But let's focus on the 'safe and sound,' shall we?

While I can't say I've conquered my fear of heights—it ain't easy overcoming heredity, folks—I did face it as best as I could. Or maybe I should say I faced it as much as I wanted to.

Or ever will again.

CHAPTER 23

Run with the Horses

―――――― ∞∞∞ ――――――

Boast on Facebook

You would be hard pressed to find a better venue, better weather, or a better host of runners and volunteers than could be found at this year's Darkside 8-Hour Run.

Let's start with the venue, the magnificent Bear Creek Farm in Moreland, Georgia. For the second year in a row Bear Creek owners Hal and Linda Barry opened up their property on Kentucky Derby Saturday so we could literally 'run with the horses.' Forty-four runners -- most of them running the entire eight hours - enjoyed the beautiful 1.02-mile asphalt loop meandering in and out of the many pastures as they were gazed upon by pairs of equine eyes throughout the day.

As for the weather: Temperatures in the high 40's at the 7 a.m. start, nothing but blue skies throughout the day and a cool breeze helping to balance things out once the temperature climbed into the low 70's in the afternoon. Ideal conditions for runners and volunteers alike, as evidenced by the many sunburnt faces noticed beneath the gazebo as awards and race mementos (pint glasses!) were handed out after the race.

As for the runners and the volunteers, what can I say but repeat something I've said time and time again: Runners are some of the finest people I know. It's my pleasure to tell you something about them.

(Please note: I had everyone sign a pre-race waiver. It was mostly standard fare—'I am participating in this event willingly and of my own accord, etc.' But I added one sentence that everyone failed to notice but I pointed out before the race officially started:

I agree not to boast about my performance on any social media with the understanding that the Race Director will take care of that detail for me after the conclusion of this event.

Now it's time for me to keep my end of the bargain.)

So, in no particular order let me tell you a little something about them:

- Runners are generous to a fault. The Darkside Running Club provided drinks and fluids for the runners and the volunteers. Entrants were asked to bring a 'community property munchie' to share with their fellow runners. At the end of the day there was still enough food left over to fill the back of a passenger van.

- Four husband-and-wife teams competed: Sandy and Danny Staggs of Livingston, Tennessee; Adamy Damaris Diaz and Don Carpenter of Greer, South Carolina; Meredith and Tim Beatty of Marietta, Georgia; and Kathleen McElhannon and Greg James of Ridgeville, South Carolina. Coincidentally, Kathleen and Greg won the unofficial 'husband & wife total mileage' competition with a combined 73.44 miles!

- Forty-four runners combined to run a cumulative 1,288.26 miles, the equivalent distance of 49+ marathons.

- Runners from six states competed: Georgia, Florida, Alabama, Tennessee, South Carolina and Minnesota. David Holmen traveled 1,141 miles from his home in Eagan, Minnesota to Moreland,

Georgia so he could celebrate his 53rd birthday by running almost 47 miles with his Darkside family. (Please note: The 44 runners ran *further* than the distance of David's trip. Who needs a plane?)

- One father and daughter competed. Together they ran 43 miles. The daughter only ran one of them, but it was really, really quick for an eight-year old. Right, Maddie?

- It was good to see Jill Floyd running well again. She'll be back to running 100-milers again before you know it. She is one tough lady.

- Our youngest runner was Angel Shoemaker, age 5 and came very close to running her age in miles.

- Our most senior runners fared quite well (ladies first): Marsha White, age 67 completed 32.64 miles and Roscoe Douglas, age 66 ran 26.52 miles.

- Don Carpenter ran a personal best for total distance.

- Jess Kurti completed a 'marathon' in the state of Georgia in her quest for the 50 States Club (accomplished by running a marathon in all 50 states).

- Susan Paraska ran a personal best for an 8-hour race. Like a fine wine…

- Lisa Grippe finished her first 50K (the first 'rung' in the ultramarathon ladder).

- Di Sha finished in second place amongst the women and ran one loop with a beer in her hand. She is my hero.

- The volunteers were WONderful: Heather and Angel Shoemaker, Molly and Isabel Wolfgram, Jill Floyd (after she knocked out just over 21 miles), Joye McElroy, Susan Lance, Caleb Torres, Anne

Rentz, Wendy Kent Mitchell (after knocking out a marathon!) and Brian Farrier. What about the Race Director, you ask? Well, the volunteers were so great I found the time to run a few loops myself, including two each with the eventual male and female winner. How did I manage to keep up with the two of them for two miles? I waited until late in the day after they both had a good 40 miles or more under their belts and the tiniest bit of fatigue was starting to set in. I wasn't born yesterday, people.

- The volunteers appreciated the two pre-sunrise containers of hot coffee, courtesy of the gracious Malissa Anderson-Strait.

- Eight runners—*eight runners* ran 40 miles or more. Four were men and four were women. Four of the women and one of the men were inducted into the Oval of Honor (40+ miles for women, 48+ miles for men). One of the women, Eileen Torres set *a new course record*. In fact, only three men have ever bettered her incredible total of 54.06 miles in the history of the event. One of those men is Ferit Toska, who won this year's race with an outstanding 56.10 miles, with over 31 of them in the first four hours of the race. It's worth mentioning Ferit is now the reigning champion of the three major Darkside events: last November's Peachtree City 50K, the Running Dead Ultra (50K) last March and now the Darkside 8-Hour. As for the other new female inductees, welcome Di Sha, Ellen Comeaux and Sarah Murphy.

- Last but not least, the Darkside 8-Hour Run will have a new Race Director next year when it is held for the 13th time. It is my honor and privilege to tell you that Joye McElroy will be taking over the reins in 2015. I hope everyone will join me in wishing her well and supporting her and the event so it will continue to be one of the most runner-friendly timed events in the world.

One last thing I want to mention: Wendy Kent Mitchell posted a photo on a certain social media on her way to the race. It was a picture of the radio dial in her car displaying the song that was playing at the time, John Cafferty's…

On the Darkside

Coincidence?

Fate?

On the Darkside, you just never know.

2014 Darkside 8-Hour Run
Bear Creek Farm, Moreland, GA

Runner	Age (in years)	State	Distance (in miles)
Ferit Toska	34	FL	56.1
Eileen Torres	43	GA	54.06
David Holmen	53	MN	46.92
Di Sha	39	GA	43.86*
John Pollard	33	GA	42.84
Ellen Comeaux	36	GA	42.84
Eric Stanley	39	GA	41.82
Sarah Murphy	48	GA	40.8
Tim Beatty	54	GA	39.78
Danny Staggs	50	TN	38.76
Ron Clay	58	GA	37.74
Kathleen McElhannon	40	SC	37.74
Susan Paraska	65	GA	36.72
Greg James	57	SC	35.7

Lisa Grippe	51	GA	33.66
Don Carpenter	56	SC	32.64
Marsha White	67	FL	32.64
Stephen Bolding	64	GA	31.62
Lynn Holtam	50	AL	31.62
Terri Chandler	64	AL	31.62
Susan Hornbuckle	50	GA	31.62
Sandy Staggs	46	TN	31.62
Paul Nyholm	41	GA	30.6
Lee Brown	56	GA	28.56
Malissa Anderson-Strait	36	GA	27.54
Jess Kurti	42	FL	27.54
Adamy Diaz-Carpenter	47	SC	27.54
Roscoe Douglas	66	GA	27.54
Tyler Brown	33	GA	26.52
Deborah Ingram	60	FL	26.52
Drina Haviland	65	GA	26.52
Meredith Beatty	42	GA	26.52
Wendy Mitchell	40	GA	26.52
Jill Floyd	51	GA	21.42
Scott Ludwig	59	GA	21.42
Kirsten Jones	45	GA	17.34
Steve Kiker	46	GA	17.34
Susan Lance	54	GA	14.28
Joye McElroy	57	GA	10.2
Anne Rentz	61	GA	10.2
Brian Farrier	55	GA	9.18
Keith Hedger	44	GA	7.14
Angel Shoemaker	5	GA	3.06

Molly Wolfgram	38	GA	2.04*
Madeleine Stanley	8	GA	1.02

Oval of Honor
Top three male finishers
Top three female finishers
*Beer-aided

CHAPTER 24

Professional Sports, R.I.P.

Sports Moratorium

After watching my beloved Florida Gators jump out to a quick 16 to 4 lead over Connecticut in the NCAA Basketball Championship's Final Four on April 5—only to then watch them play the worst 30 minutes of basketball of their entire season and lose in the tournament semifinals—I knew then and there it would be the last time I watched sports until the college football season kicked off on August 23 (even if it's only Sam Houston State playing at Eastern Washington but *hey, it's college football!*).

In other words, I was about to embark on a 140-day journey free of baseball bats, belly putters and hockey sticks. I was more than ready for a 20-week odyssey without any curve balls, low fades or slam dunks. More than anything else, I was anxious to start putting my money where my mouth is.

For the past two decades I've gradually yet steadily lost interest in and respect for professional sports. However, it's still managed to hold my attention, albeit in a much more limited manner than it did when I was a boy and a huge fan of all things Los Angeles: the Lakers, the Dodgers and the Rams. Today the Lakers are a joke, the Dodgers aren't the best baseball team in town and the Rams aren't even *in* town anymore--they moved to St. Louis a long time ago.

So for the last 20 years my ever-waning interest in professional sports has slowly eroded to the point that the next 20 weeks shouldn't be a problem, especially considering how my sports moratorium started out. After the Gators lost I refused to watch the Championship Game two nights later (I did the same thing last year, my personal boycott of the late start on a Monday night dictated by the television czars at CBS). The following night was the Atlanta Braves home opener. A vendor had invited me but through *the most unusual chain of events I ended up without a ticket and—*darn* (Facetious Font used here)—missed the game.

*A vendor invited me to the game. I turned down the invitation because my son, who was taking my grandson to his first baseball game had asked me if I wanted to go with them. I said yes.**

**A little backstory: Last September my sister who lives in Baltimore asked me if I wanted to go to the Orioles game while I was in town. My answer to her was (verbatim): 'If the guy who impales steel rods in your ears for free is on vacation that day, then yes.' And yes, I used my special Facetious Font. Her reply: 'Great; I'll get tickets!' (Lesson Learned: Facetious Font doesn't always work.)

Back to my *story. My son mistakenly thought I was using Facetious Font and knowing how much I disliked professional sports—particularly baseball, America's passed time—he didn't get me a ticket.

The very next weekend after the Gators' loss against Connecticut, the Masters was being played. There are two major golfing events I've watched religiously since I learned how to play golf almost 50 years ago: The U.S. Open and the Masters. For a perspective on how long I've been watching professional golf, the first time I saw the beauty of Augusta National the television coverage was limited to the last three holes of the third and fourth rounds. I still remember how excited I was when the coverage expanded to the *entire back nine*, even if it was still for only the third and fourth rounds.

But this year was different. This year I didn't have time for The Masters:

- First round (Thursday): I spent the day with my grandson doing anything and everything he enjoys doing.

- Second round (Friday): I worked all day and packed for my flight to take my grandson back to Fort Worth.

- Third round (Saturday): Krischan and I flew to Fort Worth and spent the day cooking on the grill and playing in the yard, ultimately spending the night together on his twin bed freshly adorned in new Ninja Turtle linens and matching Ninja Turtle bedspread.

- Fourth round (Sunday): I watched a movie with Krischan before flying back to Atlanta. I was home in time to turn on the television and catch the last hour of Masters coverage. Instead, I unpacked and sorted through Saturday's mail.

In other words, I didn't see one single shot of the Masters…and didn't miss it one bit. (Footnote: The television ratings for this year's Masters were the lowest in over 20 years. The absence of Tigers Woods is considered to be the primary reason for its poor showing. Truth be known: Tigers Woods is the primary reason I've lost interest in golf, a sport I fell in love with when I was 12 years old. I trust most of you know all about Tiger: The fire hydrant, the mistresses and his 'condition.' I can see your thought bubble: *I didn't know being a douche bag was considered a 'condition.'*)

So now that I'm over a month into my sabbatical from sports, I'll admit I haven't been able to totally absolve myself from it due to the various tickers, scrolls and alerts that bombard the television screen. For example I know that Donald Sterling, the (now former) owner of the Los Angeles Clippers made an a** of himself and received a lifetime ban from the NBA. I know that at least a half-dozen Major League Baseball players have been suspended (50 games each) for testing positive on drug tests. I know Jadeveon Clowney of the University of South Carolina was the first player chosen in the National Football League draft. Steve Spurrier, his coach at USC had made comments recently promoting Clowney's talent yet questioning his work habits, approximately the male equivalent of saying 'you don't sweat much for a fat girl.' I know they're still playing professional hockey...and it's 90 degrees here today.

But I'm proud to say I haven't watched any of it, nor do I intend to until college football is ready to kick off a little over three months from now.

In fact this year I may forego watching the only professional sport I still watch occasionally: Professional football. Let me amend that: The only professional sport I still watch occasionally once the playoffs begin.

For me it's not about who wins; it's about who loses. It's always comforting to know that at the end of the NFL season 97% of the prima donna athletes being paid millions of dollars to *play a game* will end up with the same number of Super Bowl trophies as me.

None.

Update: Father's Day weekend I spent a couple days around the house, primarily working on the yard and doing a little writing. Here's what I didn't miss:

- The Los Angeles Kings won the NHL's Stanley Cup in a short, not-what-the-Commissioner-wanted five-game series over the New York Rangers.

- The San Antonio Spurs won the NBA Championship in a short, not-what-the-Commissioner-or-ABC-television wanted five-game series over the (yawn) Miami Heat.

- Martin Kaymer, a German won golf's prestigious U.S. Open by a whopping eight shots. My favorite headline has to be this: *'2014 U.S. Open television ratings may have been lowest in history.'* As for Tiger Woods, he didn't play; he was still suffering from his 'condition.'

While three major championships were decided over the course of a weekend, I mowed the lawn, wrote a couple of chapters and joined Cindy and my son Justin for a picnic with Cindy's 88-year old dad. I think I know who the real winners were.

CHAPTER 25

Fair Weather

⟨⟨⟨⟨⟨⟩⟩⟩⟩⟩

Attend the Fayetteville Art Fair

In the middle of May you wouldn't expect to find temperatures in the mid-to-high 60's with a cool breeze thrown in for good measure to keep things comfortable. Maybe if you lived in San Diego, perhaps. But here in Georgia it's more likely to be warm and muggy at this time of the year, if not downright hot and sticky. But today was one of those days with just the right combination---lazy Sunday afternoon, great weather and wanting to take it easy after a difficult week at work—for me to say 'yes' when Cindy asked me if I wanted to attend the annual art fair in neighboring Fayetteville. After all, I've lived right next door to it for 24 years and never attended and besides, admission was free. What did I have to lose?

The very first booth Cindy and I visited offered a variety of stained glass ornaments. Cindy's eyes were immediately drawn to a stained glass peace sign, the peace sign being her Achilles Heel of Must Have's. '$25,' I thought to myself. 'Could be worse.' Then she added 'I want a stained glass window in my house someday.' There would be no peace sign today, presumably so Cindy could use it as leverage down the road when she bought an entire window made of stained glass.

The next couple of booths featured paintings that looked like they may very well have been painted by me, who has the artistic abilities of a four-year old armed with a tray of finger paint and a box of Twinkies. That is, if I ever took the time to paint parakeets and ballet slippers (I haven't).

It wasn't until we reached our fifth booth that the little plastic card in my wallet was called into action. A husband-and-wife team was selling (her) photographs converted to (his) framed prints, and they (the art, not the husband and wife) were beautiful. *(Then again, the husband and wife may have been beautiful; after all, beauty is in the eye of the beholder and since you weren't able to behold them, I really can't say if you might find them beautiful so forget I even mentioned it and just know their art was beautiful. At least in my eyes. The parakeet and ballet slippers I mentioned earlier? They couldn't possibly be considered beautiful...in anyone's eyes.)* Lots of the photographs were taken in Savannah, and I asked what else she had besides what was on display. 'Boats, lakes, birds, alligators, cobblestone streets...' I stopped her in her tracks. 'You had me at alligators,' I said as I butchered a line from *Jerry Maguire. (I collect all things University of Florida, to include anything featuring an alligator and as you will soon see, anything featuring the school colors of orange and blue. Yes, it is my Achilles Heel of Must Have's.)* She actually pulled out three photographs of alligators in a nature preserve near Savannah. It took me a solid 15 minutes before I finally settled on the photo of an alligator's head slightly above water with an orange reflection of sunlight in its eyes and a strip of green algae on its head. Cindy added a photo for friends of ours (a Christmas present bought seven months early!). The floodgates (my wallet) were now officially open for business.

We ran into Ed, our family dentist (and also a graduate of the University of Florida, a factor that may or may not have been the reason we selected him to be our family dentist 24 years ago) who thought we selected the best of the three alligator prints. I noticed Ed was overdressed for an outdoor art festival. Then again, Ed is the kind of person who would wear a suit and tie to special events; the midnight premier of a movie, for example or the grand opening of a new Hardees. *(Ed would appreciate me giving him a hard time about his attire. I do it every time he's wearing a tie while drilling on my teeth like there's gold buried in them. Besides, with my propensity for dental work I'm pretty sure I've paid for at least one of his son's college tuitions over the years.)*

I safely maneuvered my way around the next seven or eight booths—the way a soldier might navigate through a field of land mines—until Cindy found a booth featuring handmade metal jewelry. Well, maybe not so much because of the jewelry but rather because it was designed by a woman from Turkey. *(Our good friends Ferit and Gizem are from Istanbul.)* Truth be known her designs were pretty striking, and I enjoyed talking to her husband who actually made each piece (or as he told me, 'she designs, I grind'). I have to admit her husband was quite the character. A few samples:

- *We live in Alpharetta but we also have small homes in Florida and Istanbul. We don't have any money but we have a lot of homes.*

- *I played a round of golf at St. Andrews. I parred the last two holes. I have no idea what I did on the rest of the course. I still have the scorecard, but the first 16 holes are blank.*

- *I rode in a taxi in Istanbul. The driver went straight through a red light. I asked him why. He said because he didn't see anything coming.*

I dodged a few more land mines until we stumbled across a pottery tent. The man was from Florida and displayed some really attractive creations. In other words, the man was a dual threat. Four serving platters later we were on our way looking for our next victim.

It didn't take long. Another talented photographer was directly in our path and there was no way around it. And by 'it' I mean a photograph of random blue objects on an orange background *(I warned you earlier about all things orange and blue)*. The blue objects were pieces of paint and the orange background was the rusted hood of an old car the photographer stumbled across in the woods. Time to put another notch in my wallet, because this photo was *mine!*

Throughout the afternoon we saw more than one booth featuring photographs of the photogenic Starr's Mill, a favorite of local shutterbugs that is (a) about four miles from my house and (b) the centerpiece of our living room, a magnificent image of the mill with a perfect duplicate of it mirrored on the surface of the lake on which it is built. None of the photos could compare to ours, a gift from the lens of my talented friend Al last Christmas. Note: Cindy discovered a photo of another mill in one of the tents and said it 'looked familiar.' I said it was the old Rex Mill. She looked on the back of the photo and sure enough, it was Rex Mill. She asked me how I knew. *'Probably because I ran by it 3,000 or so times during the 10 years we lived in Rex.'* (Note: NOT an exaggeration; perhaps even an understatement). Moving on…

Almost done. If we can just make it past this one last vendor…TOO LATE! Cindy made her way towards one last jewelry tent the way a moth makes its way towards a light. The only difference is the moth doesn't have a wallet. Cindy did. Mine.

Final assessment: Two hours, 60 vendors, three photographs, four pieces of pottery, two pieces of jewelry and the opportunity to talk to a lot of really nice people. It was actually a pretty good deal since it didn't cost anything to get in.

Then again, it did cost me almost $400 to leave.

HALFTIME
Better Left Undone

Now that I've reached the midpoint of doing 50 things I've never done before I turn 60, I thought it might be a good time to mention a few assorted and sundry things I still haven't done as I close in on the six-month anniversary of my 59th birthday (let me know if I've lost you already).

So, in no particular order here is a list of things I've avoided doing at any time in my life, thereby making the world a better place to live:

- Split an atom. After that unfortunate chemistry experiment back in 11th grade, I'm fairly certain attempting to split an atom would be very irresponsible of me. And by 'irresponsible' I actually mean 'having catastrophic implications.'

- Tap dance, clog or perform a pirouette. After all...*why would I?*

- Inhale helium and talk like Donald Duck.

- Tame a shrew.

- Make a balloon animal. I did make one that looked like a snake or maybe a large worm but I was told it didn't count as a legitimate balloon animal because it didn't make that squeaky sound while I was making it.

112

- Wear anything red. (I discount maroon underwear as it is not technically 'red.' Also because no one should technically see my maroon underwear if I did in fact wear maroon underwear. A moot point, actually since I don't wear maroon underwear. Maroon is just too close to red for my liking. Apparently you weren't paying attention when I mentioned earlier I will not wear anything red.)

- Use a protractor.

- Eat caviar, read a romance novel or run for political office.

- Learn how to play any member of the woodwind, brass or string families of musical instruments. If I remember correctly my musical talent peaked when I was in fifth grade and I learned how to play the snare drum.

- Appreciate, understand or laugh at British humor.

- Pin the tail on the donkey. I did try to pin several 'gas leaks' on a few of our cats, however. No one ever bought it, but I *did* try.

- Get into a fistfight with any of the stars of *The Expendables,* although I did b*tch slap one of the production assistants who was in front of me at the express lane at Publix with more than 10 items (she had 13).

- Sneeze with my eyes open.

- Speak German. After working for a German company for more than 10 years and having 'Ludwig' as a last name you would think this would come naturally. Truth be known I lived in Holland for three years as a youngster and took three years of French in high school. Now when I count to 10 in a foreign language I'm pretty certain I'm doing so in three different languages. Confusing? Ciertamente!

- Count my hair.

- Perform any repairs involving electricity. I saw someone who 'knew what he was doing' fly across my kitchen after removing a kitchen outlet the stove was hooked up to and receiving a butt load of kilowatts. I'm smart enough to know I *don't* know what I'm doing. I'm also smart enough to know electricity is not my friend.

- Give a telephone marketer a fighting chance. Ask around; they'll tell you I can be a real a**, especially the ones who call the minute I get home from work, the minute I hit the sack and lest I forget, God-have-mercy-on-the-souls of those who call me on my cell phone.

- Exceed the speed of light or solve a Rubik's Cube. I mention both since my chance of doing either one is about the same. I may as well add 'complement the University of Georgia' while I'm at it.

- Spontaneously combust.

CHAPTER 26

Never Too Old for Young

<hr>

Discover the Genius of Neil Young

After listening to the first couple of lines of several Neil Young songs on satellite radio—while finding his voice fascinating yet never listening to any of them all the way through, I decided to take the plunge and buy a copy of his Greatest Hits (capitalized for a reason) to see what I'd been missing out on the past four decades.

It didn't take long for me to realize what I'd been missing out on: Quite a bit.

Back in high school the only song by Neil Young I can recall is *Old Man*. At the time I had a hard time connecting with it; after all, I was still several years shy of turning 20. 'Old man' and Neil Young were simply not on my radar.

It is now. I'm glad I finally found the time to discover the musical genius of one of the finest musicians of my generation ... although to be honest I barely knew he existed at the time. I spent most of my high school afternoons listening over and over (and over) to Grand Funk Railroad's *Live Album*. Back then it was my absolute favorite compilation of music and I would bet my entire CD collection (yes, I have *Grand Funk Live Album* on CD!) no one has listened to the album more than I have (did you notice the special DEAD SERIOUS font?). The only thing I knew about Neil Young is he played with Crosby, Stills and Nash for a short period of time. I thought CS&N were tossing him a biscuit, so to speak. After listening to his Greatest Hits, I believe I had it wrong: Neil Young was doing CS&N a favor playing with *them*. I stand corrected: Neil Young was literally gracing them with his presence.

I am so *stoked* with Neil Young's Greatest Hits that I want to tell you about each song—all 16 of them—so you'll be as *stoked* as I am and want to give it a listen. You can tell I'm *stoked* because I haven't used the word 'stoked' since the last time I did a 360 on a skateboard. Give me a second to cue up my CD player.

I am now pressing 'play.'

- *Down by the River* – Young's mesmerizing voice transitions into several virtuoso guitar performances that will make you want to burn incense and light up like you did when you heard *Dark Side of the Moon* for the first time. (Note: If you weren't around in 1973 please disregard. Unless you live in Colorado or Washington.) Bonus: Haunting bass riffs abound.

- *Cowgirl in the Sand* – More of the same. Ten minutes worth, to be exact. I'm in heaven…free of anything you can legally obtain in Colorado or Washington, of course. I like this song so much I could put it on 'repeat' until marijuana is legalized in Georgia.

- *Cinnamon Girl* – Catchy bass riff. I remember naming the artist and title of this song correctly at our weekly music trivia competition. Twice. Reading the liner notes I now know the year it was released as well: 1969. I remember 1969: I was listening to the Doors, Tommy James and the Shondells and the theme from *Hawaii 5-0*.

- *Helpless* – It's a pretty catchy tune for a slow ballad.

- *After the Gold Rush* – Like *Helpless*, only better. God, I love this man's voice. The accompaniment of a brass instrument (the one that sounds like a melodic elephant's mating call) adds a nice touch.

- *Only Love can Break your Heart* – The only thing that could make this song—another ballad—even better would be if there was a choir singing in the background. The song deserves a choir singing in the background. You'll just have to imagine, same as I did.

- *Southern Man* – I've read that some call Neil Young 'the Godfather of Grunge.' Now I understand. Pearl Jam, Soundgarten, Nirvana—back of the line, please.

- *Ohio* – A protest song written by Neil Young (and performed by CSN&Y, the 'Y' representing NEIL YOUNG!) in reaction to the Kent State shootings in 1970. Maybe the most recognizable Neil Young lyric of all time: *'Four dead in O-HI-O.'*

- *The Needle and the Damage Done* – The voice...the acoustic guitar...the lyrics *('I watched the needle take another man...')*. Neil Young describes the descent into heroin addiction (and in some cases, death) of musicians he knew. Wow. Simply... *Wow.*

- *Old Man* – Neil Young's catchy tune compares a young man's life to an old man's and points out he has essentially the same needs. OK, so I'm a little late to the party, but (a) I get it and (b) I realized I've always liked the song in a distant kind of way. I guess deep down inside I knew what the years had in store for me.

- *Heart of Gold* – Neil Young's prowess with the harmonica is evident throughout the song. Gee, I wonder if he's touring in this area anytime soon...

- *Like a Hurricane* – This has simply got to be *THE ABSOLUTE COOLEST SONG EVER!!!* Over eight minutes of coolness. This CD will be giving the boys from Grand Funk Railroad a run for their money before it's all over. If you listen to the song closely you'll hear Young's guitar screaming for mercy. More than once.

- *Comes a Time* – Even Grand Funk had its *Some Kind of Wonderful*. I'm using my get-out-of-jail-free card for this one.

- *Hey Hey My My (Into the Black)* – I hereby nominate Neil Young as Godfather of Kick-Ass Guitar Licks. Can I get a second?

- *Rockin' in the Free World* – Never mind; this song is the only 'second' I need.

- *Harvest Moon* – The first time I heard this song I thought to myself: *'This is the absolute best love song I've ever heard in my life.'* I've listened to it enough in the past 24 hours to know that you would have a hard time proving me wrong.

While I'm sad I missed out on the art, the talent and the absolute *magic* of Neil Young for over 40 years, I'm glad I have it to look forward to from this point on. I'm just sorry it took me so long to discover.

But better late than never. I'm sure Neil Young has written a song about that somewhere along the line.

CHAPTER 27

The Senoia Road Six

―⚬―

Become a Foster Parent for Kittens

I host running events on New Year's Day, Memorial Day and Labor Day. Several years ago my friend Susan brought a couple of kittens she was fostering to the event on Labor Day. My wife Cindy came to the park that day and before I knew what hit me 'Moe' (Hawaiian for 'sleep' and boy does the name fit) became the fourth feline in the Ludwig family. Moe is a male orange tabby who has grown into a rather large cat. How best to describe his size? Let's just say he is to a Shetland pony what a Shetland pony is to a horse. Cindy and I swore to each other that very day that Moe would be the last stray kitten we would take into our home.

A little over a year later Cindy and I were returning to our hotel after I ran a marathon in Morganton, North Carolina when a silver tabby walked out from under a car and brushed up against my leg. I went to the convenience store for a can of cat food and served it along with a cup of water to the obviously very hungry and very thirsty kitten. Cindy and I decided we would take the kitten back to Georgia with us and do what Susan does: Become foster parents for the kitten until we found it a Forever Home. As good as it sounds as I write it to this day I ask myself: What could possibly go wrong? How about this:

> *We couldn't tell if the kitten was a boy or a girl. So Cindy says*
> *'Why don't we call it Morgan? That could be a boy or a girl's*
> *name and after all, we found the kitten in Morganton.'*

If there's one thing I know to be true, it is this: Once you name a kitten, the kitten is yours for life.

So if you haven't been keeping score at home, that puts the tally at two humans and five felines in the Ludwig household. The balance of power is now with those who have their litter boxes cleaned every morning by the person with a job, apparently so he can afford cat food and lots and lots of kitty litter.

This past Saturday morning Al, Amanda and I went for our usual 10-mile run in Fayetteville. We were on Old Senoia Road and saw something that caught our attention on the edge of the asphalt (it was about 5:45 a.m. so it was still dark outside). We aimed our flashlights at the crescent-shaped crack in the road and found something that immediately caused our three rapidly-beating hearts to melt: Six tiny, shivering, wide-eyed kittens huddled together, terrified of what might happen to them next. The thought of 'who could have done such a terrible thing' didn't even cross our minds; we were too concerned for the welfare of the kittens.

So let me describe the situation as best as I can: We ran to Al's house as hard as we could (the only tabby in the litter was chasing after us—we had to 'shoo' him back if in fact shoo-ing kittens actually works) to get our cars so we could return to Old Senoia Road and rescue them. Fortunately Amanda had a cardboard box and several old sweatshirts destined for good will in her car which we used to place the five quivering (Cold? Afraid? Both?) kittens into. Wait...*five?* Who's missing? Of course, the gray tabby that was chasing after us (Note: Shoo-ing kittens does in fact *not* work)!

Amanda and I (Al had to leave for work) spent a good 45 minutes searching for the missing feline. No luck...until a husband and wife who had been walking in the park across the street from the recreation complex we had been scouring returned to the parking lot and mentioned they noticed a cat lurching beneath their vehicle (Note: I had already looked under every vehicle parked at the complex and didn't see it). Amanda got down on all fours, looked under the car and found the tabby inside the rim of the wheel and draped over the back axle, hissing like a banshee. Now one of them had a name: Axle, complements of Amanda. Once we had all six kittens corralled, we had to decide what to do next.

I texted a photograph I had taken of the five (pre-Axle) kittens to my wife's cell phone, called her at home and told her to look at the photo and call me back. Two minutes later she called back: 'Ahhhhhh...' The kittens now had Cindy in their back pockets along with Amanda, Al and I. What now?

For starters, I posted the photo on my Facebook page with the caption 'Sometimes you find the neatest things on your morning run.' The power of social media immediately went to work. (If I would have had time to give it more thought I would have created a Facebook page for the Senoia Road Six.) My post was getting more 'likes' and more 'shares' than anything I've ever posted before. Now if I can only find some Forever Homes for the little ones...

I took them home and Cindy and I set up our screened-in back porch as their temporary living quarters, playground, dining area and bathroom. Equipped with large bowls of food and water and a litter box on loan from our own five cats, the kittens spent the day eating, drinking, frolicking (a combination game of tag/leap frog that Cindy coined just the right word for: 'Adorable') and using everything that wasn't a litter box for a bathroom. They also took a couple naps, each time all six of them resembling a pile of fuzzy pick-up sticks, just as we had found them earlier in the day.

I made a trip to the bank and showed my favorite teller Stephanie the photo of the kittens. I asked her if she was interested in having one of them. 'I might be.' Several hours later I got a message from her on Facebook asking if I would be home today and could she come by and see the kittens? Stephanie could have also asked me if I'd cook her dinner and wash her car if she came by and gotten the same answer: YES!

So what now? Stephanie would want to see the kittens in their 'natural habitat,' the back porch. So we had to do something about the minefield of poo and that awful smell in the air, not the greatest selling point for kitten adoptions. For the next hour Cindy and I scraped *(Note: I can clean up my own cats' poo with no problems. However, cleaning up another cat's poo is a different story. Parents—Do you know how you can stomach cleaning up your infant's vomit but simply seeing someone else's infant vomiting makes you sick? It works that way with kitten poo as well.)*, scrubbed and shined for Stephanie's visit. For good measure we lit a scented candle to freshen the air; if not freshen it then at least to disguise it.

Later Saturday afternoon Stephanie and her daughter stopped by and it wasn't long before 'Ash,' the solid gray kitten that I would have chosen if I had to choose just one had his Forever Home.

All day long the next day I continued to correspond with people on Facebook about the kittens. Susan (trained in the veterinary sciences as well as being arguably the World's Greatest Pet Foster Parent) ran with me that morning and after our run came in to identify the age (eight weeks) and gender (three males, two females) of the remaining five kittens. 'Axle' was a boy, 'Sta-Puft' (his face resembled that of a blowfish and/or the marshmallow monster in *Ghostbusters*) was a boy, 'Stripe' (gray with a thin white stripe on the bridge of her nose) was a girl, 'Suzie' (she looked just like a cat I had when I was 10 years old) was a girl and 'Highlight' (gray with a predominately white face) was a boy. (Note: The only name I said aloud was Axle—whom Amanda named and Sta-Puft—whom I named but wouldn't really name him that were he mine because it just sounds silly...even if it *was* appropriate!)

Monday was Memorial Day. A day for another of my holiday running events, like the one I held on Labor Day several years ago when Moe joined our family. It was now time for some cosmic karma to take place. Let's see if 'paying it forward' actually paid off.

Let me summarize the day by saying Cindy and I truly had karma on our side, paying it forward *does* pay off and as I've known for many, many years; runners are some of the finest people on the planet. Memorial Day couldn't have been more memorable: The rest of the Senoia Road Six found their Forever Homes.

'Highlight' was adopted by a young couple who stumbled upon our group of runners on their way to a picnic-for-two by the lake. The second the woman made eye contact with the white-faced kitten I knew it had a new home; it was after a minute or two of convincing her husband in Spanish that he knew as well. Later I took a small bag of kitten food and a couple of kitten toys (Cindy's idea) to them and I could tell by the way the woman was holding the kitten in her arms it was a good fit for the both of them. I noticed the look on the face of her husband; it was obviously a good fit for him as well.

As you already know, 'Ash' was adopted by my friend from the bank. Stephanie, I'm so glad 'Oliver is now part of your family.

'Suzy' was adopted by a wonderful couple from Greenville, South Carolina. Don and Adamy, I'm so glad 'Amy' is now part of your family.

'Stripe' was adopted by a young lady from the north side of Atlanta who is new to our running group. Veronica, I'm so glad 'Chloe' is now part of your family.

'Axle' and 'Sta-puft' were both adopted by a young lady, also from the north side of Atlanta and a veteran of our running group. Heather, I'm so glad 'Ares' and 'Nebula' are now part of your family. I know your daughter Angel must be thrilled.

Later in the afternoon all of the new 'parents' (sans the Mexican couple, because I didn't get their name; just a photo of them with the kitten) posted photos on Facebook of their new additions.

Although I felt my heart melting all over again, this time it was for a different reason:

The Senoia Road Six had found their Forever Homes.

Postscript: Each year the Darkside Running Club picks a specific race and donates up to $1,000 to be divided amongst members of the club participating in the race.

A couple days after Memorial Day I recommended to the club we donate this year's sponsorship money amongst the new parents of the Senoia Road Six for initial trips to the veterinarian, kitten food and kitty litter.

I am proud to report that there were no objections, and a considerably large number of written endorsements.

Updates: Ares and Nebula have relocated to Wisconsin where they are now living with Heather's relatives. Heather, unbeknownst to her when she adopted the two kittens has a severe allergy to cats; it was with great sadness she had to give up custody.

I received this Christmas letter from Amy Darkside:

Dear Uncle Scott and Aunt Cindy:

Thanks for allowing my humans to borrow your pet carrier to bring me home with them. So far I've had a great time since becoming part of their family. I don't understand why the other cats are always annoyed with me...even though I've managed to blend in.

I like playing with Misty the calico, even when she pretends not to like me. And I've wondered why Dusty the gray tabby refuses to let me nurse her. Now, Zombie is a different story: I can get close to him and kiss him or we can play fight. He even tried to sneak into this box to come visit you. (Note: The letter came in a cardboard box with the pet carrier I loaned Don and Adamy, a framed collage of 'all things Amy,' and a photo of Zombie the cat hiding inside the box before it was sealed.)

All in all, I've found a good place to call home thanks to you. Thanks for rescuing me and insisting that I come home with these humans. They are all right.

Much love,
Amy Darkside

P.S. Do you know what ADHD is? Just wondering, 'cause
I hear my humans say that to me sometimes.

CHAPTER 28

Long Way to Run

— ◈◈◈ —

Run my 135,000th Mile

Let's pretend a smooth asphalt road completely encircles the earth and follows the exact path of the equator. Now imagine my home in Peachtree City, Georgia is located on that road *(it's not, but we're pretending, remember?)*.

Now pretend I left my house for a run heading east and I ran every mile I've ever run in my life all at once without stopping.

If all of these things were true, then I would have been running through Jhang, Pakistan this year on the last day of May.

Actually, if I never strayed from that imaginary path on the equator I would have been running through Jhang for the *sixth* time, as that was the day I ran my 135,000th lifetime mile.

As you may have already gathered I have kept pretty diligent records of my running for the past 35+ years. My running logs have at least one entry every single day since November 30, 1978. The last day I failed to run—November 29, 1978—was due to an unfortunate problem with my stomach caused by something I inflicted on myself the day before. It could have been one of two things: (1) Running 13 miles to win a bet with my college professor who knew the longest distance I ever ran was only eight miles, or (2) drinking a couple of celebratory pitchers of beer afterwards, complements of my college professor paying off his lost wager. Now that I think about it, it was probably a little bit of both.

I've been a slave to numbers for as long as I can remember. I have always set mileage goals for myself: Weekly, monthly and yearly. In my prime if I set a goal of running 90 miles in a week, I would 'load up' on the front end of the week to ensure that by the time the week was drawing to a close I would be assured of reaching my target. Inevitably this led to weeks of 100 or more miles because I would usually finish the week the same way it started: With high mileage. *(You can imagine the results when this philosophy is extended into months and years of running. That being said 135,000 miles in 35 years should really come as no surprise.)*

As for being a slave to numbers, I have historically tried to tie in 'milestone mileage' plateaus with something of significance in my running career. For instance I reached 100,000 lifetime miles as I crossed the finish line of the 2005 Atlanta Marathon (one of my favorite races) and 125,000 miles on the 50-yard line of Florida Field in 2011 amidst a welcoming entourage consisting of my wife, the University of Florida cheerleaders and what-Gator-celebration-would-be-without school mascots Albert and Alberta Alligator.

So I meticulously planned my week leading up to the culmination of running my 135,000[th] mile as I wanted it to be at the exact same spot where one week earlier Al, Amanda and I found six abandoned kittens on the side of the road. It required a 20-mile run on Monday and a total of 36 miles the rest of the week, but it was well worth the effort. When Al, Amanda and I reached the nine-mile mark of our 10-mile Saturday morning run, we stopped to let the moment soak in. One hundred and thirty-five thousand miles. The adoption of all six kittens less than a week ago. Another exhilarating, never-taken-for-granted run in the country. Good health. Camaraderie. Physical fitness. Friendship. The simplicity and purity of running.

The moment was special for a lot of reasons. It made me think of all the other special moments in my life, all of which I could affix a number to if I had the urge *(that number being my lifetime running mileage at that point in time):*

- The day Cindy and I moved from Florida to Georgia.
- The births of both of our sons.
- The deaths of Cindy's parents.
- The deaths of my parents.
- The birth of our grandson.
- The day we moved into our new house in Peachtree City.
- The days both of our sons graduated from high school and for one of them, college.
- The day I said goodbye to a company I was with for 24 years.
- The day I said hello to a company I have been with ever since.

But assigning a number to these moments would be the wrong thing to do. You can't put a number, *any* number—whether it be mileage, value or importance on a scale of one-to-ten—on the moments that define your life.

With that thought in mind I'm going to try my very best to quit placing numerical goals on myself. Lord knows I've tried cutting back on my mileage over the years but I'll be the first to tell you the success has been negligible. If whether or not I've been successful at 'cutting back' was up for debate, a novice debater might argue I have indeed been running fewer miles the past couple of years and therefore have successfully 'cut back.' However, a veteran debater might concede I'm running fewer miles but that I'm still spending as much time on the roads since I'm running considerably slower than in years past and therefore have not technically 'cut back.'

However, a *master* debater could bring the whole matter to an abrupt close by pointing out the obvious: Successfully 'cutting back' requires less mileage AND less time spent running. *(Note: There is no such thing as a 'master debater.' I just wanted to use it in print to see if it was as much fun reading it as it was hearing it said out loud. Footnote to note: It's not.)*

So today I vow to quit placing mileage goals on myself. I don't need the stress, the pressure or the demand of running X miles each week, each month or each year.

As long as I can run my 150,000[th] lifetime mile by the time I turn 65…

Postscript: The evening of May 31st Cindy and I attended a Collective Soul concert. The encore consisted of two songs: *Shine* followed by the finale *Run*. You may be familiar with the last line of the song, which is repeated several times before the song comes to an end:

Have I got a long way to run?

Karma can be a bitch. Or perhaps my ally. Sometimes it's hard to tell.

It's up for debate.

Postscript: Before the end of the year I passed 137,000 lifetime miles. I also passed 60 lifetime years. It made me wonder if 150,000 miles by age 65 was still realistic. It also made me wonder why I keep setting numerical goals on myself that don't matter to anyone in the world but me. Old habits die hard.

CHAPTER 29

Letting Go

⟨⟨⟨∞⟩⟩⟩

Attempt a World Record

A little over seven-and-a-half tons.

Surely that will be enough to get me into the *Guinness Book of World Records*.

For what, you ask?

For giving 15,000 pounds back to nature over the course of the last five decades or so.

15,000 pounds of *what*, you ask?

Here's the tricky part. If you have to ask, you probably don't want to know.

Note: If this applies to you—*if YOU have to ask*—you can now be excused.

If you *don't* have to ask that can only mean you already know and if that's the case-- this story is for you.

*'So tell me, Scott. Exactly how do you figure you're responsible for putting
100 times your body weight back into the soil?'*

Great question. You may want to follow along with a calculator while I explain.

I've run a little over 135,000 miles over the past soon-to-be 36 years. Based on more than 18,000 hours of personal running experience I have deduced that I stop to answer Nature's Call approximately once every 3.5 miles. In other words my runs have been interrupted well over 38,000 times. My personal high stands at eleven stops during one particularly memorable 20-mile run (one stop for every 1.82 miles!). I attribute that particular performance to three things: (1) The consumption of several beers the night before the run; (2) the consumption of two cups of coffee the morning of the run and (3) temperatures in the low 20's during the three hours of the run. Basketball guru Phil Jackson might refer to that as my 'triangle offense' because when all three of these things are aligned, I'm bound to score at any moment; quite often in flurries.

That brings me to the next number you may now enter into your calculator: Six, representing the approximate weight in ounces of my average 'score.' How do I know this? When I ran across Death Valley 11 summers ago my 'output' was monitored closely to ensure my vital organs were functioning. What better way to keep tabs on my kidneys than by measuring the yellow (and later yellow-orange and ultimately orange-red) fluid coming out of me? So believe me when I tell you I know what six ounces feels like on the way out; 40,000 reps will do that to a person.

(At this time those of you who have literally been using a calculator will realize I've now accounted for those 15,000 pounds. However there remain more than 1,000 reps unaccounted for. Patience.)

So at this point my guestimate of slightly more than 38,000 pit stops leaves me a little bit short of 40,000. What I haven't yet figured into the equation is the number of times Nature Called that was in no way related to running. For example all of the band parties at my fraternity house during my undergraduate college years when I would wander next door and relieve myself on the side of the neighboring house occupied by those snooty brothers of Alpha Tau Omega. Or those times at the beach when it was perfectly acceptable to take care of business in the ocean since it wasn't like doing the same thing in a chlorinated swimming pool where the slight colorization of the water would be a dead give-away.

So a couple of indiscretions here, a couple of indiscretions there and before you know it—BAM!—40,000! As you might expect anyone with 40,000 'calls of the wild' will have a story or two to tell. I, on the other hand have more than a story or two but for the sake of brevity and so I don't say anything that could still be looked upon as 'within the statute of limitations' I'll simply share my favorite (and one I'm not responsible for):

I was leading the four-and-a-half-hour pace group at the Mercedes Marathon in Birmingham, Alabama several years ago. I had a small group of 10 or 12 runners and at one point early in the race we were running through the campus of the University of Alabama at Birmingham. Suddenly I found myself in need of finding a bush to water, if you know what I mean. I handed the pace group leader sign to 'Charlie' and told him to keep the runners on pace and that I would be right back. I ran across some grass and found some bushes on the side of a building with a large plate glass window in front, facing the runners passing by. The window was tinted so that when you looked at it directly from the outside you couldn't see in, but you *could* see your reflection; however anyone inside the building had no trouble seeing out. My secluded spot in the bushes allowed me to see into the building from an angle, and I could see that behind the window were 20 or more students seated at their desks directly facing the window. I then glanced back to see where Charlie and my pace group were, only to discover Charlie standing directly in front of the plate glass window and—in all his glory—doing exactly what I was doing in the bushes with one exception:

> *He was doing it all over the plate glass window, and*
> *judging by his reaction at seeing his reflection in the*
> *window apparently very proud of his performance.*

What Charlie failed to see were the reactions of the UAB students as they stared intently—their eyes WIDE OPEN--as Charlie took care of business.

Once Charlie and I rejoined the other runners I mentioned to him there were students behind the plate glass window and that he definitely had their attention. He didn't bat an eye. Charlie would have made a great fraternity brother.

Charlie's indiscretion didn't come back to haunt him, fortunate considering he was wearing his race number pinned on the front of his shirt and it would have been very easy for the students to identify the crazed window washer to the authorities.

Again, that last story was about CHARLIE. It wasn't about SCOTT. I have to make that distinction perfectly clear since I don't know what the statute of limitations is for that kind of thing.

Postscript: I submitted this to the good people at the *Guinness Book of World Records*. I'm not holding my breath on getting a response, but I do know I'm adding to that 40,000 each and every day.

Just in case they *do* come calling.

CHAPTER 30

Just Words

———— ∞ ————

Compose a Love Letter to my Wife

I wrote this for Cindy for our 37ᵗʰ wedding anniversary.

Just (juhst):
Only, merely (adverb)
True, deserved (adjective)

Word (werd):
A single distinct meaningful element of speech or writing (noun)

....

Sometimes the heart sees what is invisible to the eye.

*To the world you may be one person, but to
one person you may be the world.*

When I am with you, the only place I want to be is closer.

Who ever loved that loved not at first sight?

The first time I ever saw you I knew you were the one. I believe you knew it as well; in fact you admitted as much when you signed my annual during our senior year in high school. I bet you thought I'd forgotten. I haven't.

Love has been written about since the beginning of time. Love makes the world go round. Love is a many-splendored thing. Love is composed of a single soul inhabiting two bodies.

A single soul inhabiting two bodies—isn't that what we've always been looking for?

Somehow we haven't been able to completely find it yet, because that little thing known as *life* always seems to get in the way. Juggling two full time careers, raising two children, maintaining a household and being grandparents consumes a great deal of our time; time we're not always able to spend together.

But those days of just you and I are coming. One day we'll be retiring and able to spend time doing other things when we *want* to—not because we *have* to. When that day comes the final—the *best* chapter of our lives will begin.

We'll sit on the porch and reminisce about our first date, our first child and our first grandchild. We'll lie by the fireplace and laugh about the fun times putting snow chains on the tires outside of Boone, eating pears in Sarajevo and discovering Justin skied off the side of that mountain in Park City. We'll sit in the back yard and flash back to our college years and the good times with Gator football, disco dancing and married housing. We'll lie in bed and take a journey back in time to the relaxing mountains of North Carolina, the quaint little villages of Germany and the gentle ocean breezes of Maui.

Even though we already have a lifetime of memories to share, I have every reason to believe the best is yet to come.

I knew in high school I wanted to spend my life with you…grow old with you…love you for the rest of my life. You were my high school sweetheart then, and you're my high school sweetheart now.

I promised you then and I promise you now: I will always love you. You are the very best thing that's ever happened to me. I may not always show it, I may not always say it, but I know in my heart it's true.

I may never be able to build you a castle.

I may never be able to write 'I love you' in the sky.

I may never be able to fly you to the moon.

But I'll always be able to tell you how much I love you, because for that all I need are words.

Postscript: For our anniversary Cindy had orange and blue flowers sent to my office. They were 'Gator' flowers. Advantage: Cindy.

CHAPTER 31

Toot my own Horn

⎯⎯⎯⎯⎯⎯ ⚭ ⎯⎯⎯⎯⎯⎯

Self-Promote

Spurred on by the success Cindy and I had finding homes for all six kittens found on Old Senoia Road over the Memorial Day weekend, a part of me that was dormant (translation: never existed) for much too long came alive. I realized that if there was something I truly believed in (in this case the welfare of six orphaned kittens) I could indeed be a bona fide salesman.

Let me back up for a moment. When I was a Scout (Cub, Boy—can't remember for certain; immaterial, really) many years ago it seemed like I spent more time selling chocolate-covered Macadamia nuts door-to-door (our family was living on Oahu at the time) than I did pitching a tent or sitting by a campfire sticking my fingers into cans of Vienna sausages. In fact I'm pretty sure I earned a merit badge for Fundraising along the way. But I hated every second of it. I don't know what I hated more: Asking people to part with their hard-earned money for some ridiculously overpriced candy, or the fact that I was terrible at it. I was such a bad salesman I may as well have been selling lighter fluid to Smokey the Bear because the answer was always the same: No.

But as I said, finding homes for the six kittens proved I *could* be a salesman. I just need a product I believe in.

Flash forward to a couple (four) decades later. I had recently been recruited to endorse a particular brand of insoles for runners. The pay was going to be commensurate with the pay I received for giving presentations to runners, writing regular columns for two regional running publications and serving as President of the Darkside Running Club; in other words, gratis. The marketing department of the insole company knew I had written (at that time) three books about running and was going to be running in South Africa's Comrades Marathon soon. Coincidentally the insole company was located in Johannesburg, South Africa—where I would be flying into before heading over to Durban for the start of the race.

So the insole company made me an offer I couldn't refuse.

'If we pick you up at the Johannesburg airport and drive you to your lodging, would you mind signing 50 copies of *A Few Degrees from Hell* (my third book) so we can use it in a promotional campaign?'

Why yes, you certainly may.

So the night Susan Lance and I flew into Johannesburg we met up with 'Lutz' and his business partner and they drive us to our armed and impenetrable bed and breakfast in the middle of downtown Johannesburg. And yes, I did mean to say 'armed and impenetrable' (have you ever *been* to Johannesburg?) and the analogy to a fortress is most definitely intentional. I signed 50 copies of my book and two days later I was interviewed by a reporter from South Africa's *Modern Athlete* magazine for their special Comrades Marathon edition. As I understood it, I was supposed to appear on the cover. However as it turned out a local 'biggest loser' appeared on the cover (but in his defense, he *did* lose more weight than I'm currently lugging around...), but I did get a two-page spread near the front of the magazine—with plenty of photographs and a rather conspicuous ad for the insole I was promoting.

Although *A Few Degrees from Hell* had been selling reasonably well leading up to Comrades, afterwards sales went to a whole new level. It was less than a year later that a 'literary headhunter' gave me a call asking me if I'd be interested in selling the rights to the book to a publisher located in Aachen,

Germany. I asked him how he knew of my book and he said the publisher tasked him with finding a running narrative book worthy of publication. Apparently my book was appearing on whatever tracking mechanism there is in place to determine which books were selling reasonably well in the self-publishing world, and mine apparently caught his attention.

So after selling more than 4,000 copies of *A Few Degrees from Hell* with little or no marketing or promotion and after considerable time spent contemplating over whether or not to give the rights to my book to someone else, I decided it was time for me to 'go global.' After the first eight months with my new publisher an additional 900 copies of the book were sold. *(Did I mention I also signed over the movie rights to my book—should it in fact be turned into a movie? I mention it because I signed over the movie rights to my book in case it is turned into a movie. Not that the thought of it makes my head swell or anything.)*

Which brings me to what I did today: I began a one-person promotional campaign for my two latest books on Facebook (for *Buy the Book* Part 1 and *Buy the Book* Part 2). Here's what I posted:

I've never been known to be a salesman or a marketer, but I do have an offer that (I'm hoping) 10 of you can't refuse:

The first 10 Facebook friends who send me a private message with their home address will receive a copy of Buy the Book! (either Part 1 or Part 2—no promises). There are only three conditions:

1. *You have to read the entire book within five weeks of receipt (no skimming and no buying a copy of their respective CliffNotes).*

2. *You then have to post a review of the book on Amazon (good, bad, indifferent—just be honest.).*

3. *You have to post a review on Facebook (again—good, bad, indifferent).*

Why am I doing this? Let's just say I believe in the law of geometric progression. And I believe you'll enjoy the books.

Believe me when I say I would have never considered doing something this bold if it wasn't something I truly believed in. But I do believe anyone who reads my books will enjoy them; I wouldn't say so if I didn't. As for the law of geometric progression, I'm counting on the 10 people reading the books to tell 10 of their friends about them who will then read the books and then tell 10 of *their* friends...

I had my 10 commitments within 24 hours. My sales pitch is over; now let's see what the law of geometric progression can do.

Postscript: You might have noticed my name hasn't made the New York Times Best Seller list. Yet.

CHAPTER 32

Sir Edmund Hillary has nothing to Fear

———— ∞∞∞ ————

Hike to the Mountain Top

My longtime friend Al is an optometrist who lives about 10 miles from me five days out of the week. The other two days he lives about 160 miles away...in his cabin in the mountain overlooking Lake Nantahala in Macon County, North Carolina. It is his retreat, his home-away-from-home and his favorite place to engage in three of his favorite activities: photography, painting and hiking.

Al's favorite hiking route is the five-mile round trip from Wayah Gap to Siler Bald, the first half requiring a climb of almost 1,300 feet in elevation. He's made the hike well over 100 times, and with Cindy away in New York for the weekend I thought it was the opportune time for me to accompany Al to his cabin and make my initial hike to Siler Bald.

Al has a routine he religiously follows on his weekend getaways and I didn't want to interfere, so the first thing we did on the drive to the mountains was stop at Moe's for dinner. (I forgot to mention another of Al's favorite activities: Eating.) Al and I both ordered a vegan burrito, served with a generous helping of tortilla chips and as-much-as-you-need salsa. As I sat across from him I couldn't help but notice how much food was stockpiled on his tray and that he was shoveling food into his mouth so fast that I'm pretty I saw him eat a napkin.

Once we got to the cabin we had a couple of beers (not part of Al's normal routine, nor mine for that matter) and called it a night around 10 p.m. We were up at 4 the next morning to begin our hike to Siler Bald. But first, Al wanted me to get my run in so he laid out the following game plan:

- Al drops me off at the base of the mountain and drives *up* the 4.3-mile dirt road up to Wayah Bald to take photographs of the sunrise.
- I run *up* the 4.3-mile dirt road up to Wayah Bald to get my run in for the day.
- We drive *down* the 4.3-mile dirt road and cross the road over to Wayah Gap for our joint hike to Siler Bald.

So at 5:30 a.m. and armed with a handheld flashlight I began the climb to Wayah Bald. Portions of the road were so hilly I was forced to interrupt my run by walking a step or two (in a land where one step = one mile). Once I made it to the top I told Al I wanted to cash in on my reward for running uphill by starting to run back *downhill*; you know, for the easy part.

Well, there once was a time when running downhill was 'the easy part.' Unfortunately that time was not in this century. I had only run a little over a mile on the once-upon-a-time easy part when Al pulled up in the car and told me to get inside. No complaints from me.

We made our way over to Wayah Gap to begin our ascent to Siler Bald. Al took along a pair of hiking poles and a backpack; I took along a cell phone and a camera. It wasn't difficult for anyone crossing our paths to know which one of us was the rookie.

I followed Al for a little more than an hour through the Nantahala Forest and I'm proud to report we made the ascent without incident. No falls, no cuts, no bruises and no brushes with death. In fact the only part of the climb that caused me to break out in a cold sweat was when we came upon a gorge and had to walk across two logs stretched from one side of the gorge to the other. I just made sure not to look down at the impending 3,000-foot drop to the bed of boulders directly beneath us (in a land where one foot = one millimeter and boulders are actually pebbles). The path was painted spectacularly in every shade of green imaginable. We spent some time at the top—Siler Bald, elevation 5,216 feet—and took several photographs as Al pointed out mountains in the distance in the neighboring states of Georgia and Tennessee. Al showed me the area where he spread his brother's ashes several years earlier and mentioned what a windy day it had been and that some of the ashes had blown back in his face. I mentioned he might be the only person to ever snort a member of his own family (now might be a good time to mention Al and I share a similar sense of humor).

I took the lead on the descent, me being a veteran of the route and all. At one point we heard a creature moving about in the foliage: Al thought it was a squirrel while I was pretty sure it was a polar bear. In retrospect I believe Al was probably right because if it were a polar bear the white fur would have stuck out like a sore thumb amongst all that green.

Right after that Al took the lead for the remaining half-mile or so. I'm glad he did so he didn't have to see my impromptu balancing act when my right foot slid off of a rock. Imagine this for a moment (if you're Nadia Comaneci please skip ahead to the next paragraph):

- You're on one of those razor-thin balance beams in a pair of trail shoes, nervously trying to maintain your balance.

- Some wise guy sticks his thumb in your thigh, causing you to flinch.

- The flinch leads to a desperate flailing of both arms—something you might see in an old Bugs Bunny cartoon—that goes on for what seems like a minute or more before you finally regain your balance...and ultimately your dignity.

- You make sure the expression on your face is one of 'nothing to look at here; just move along.'

However, the nervous perspiration all over your face totally blows your cover. (Now might be a good time to share that Al and I have a similar sense of balance, giving him no room to either criticize or comment and I of course would do the same for him; in fact I *have* done the same for him—many times. As he has for me—also many times.)

A couple other topics of conversation in the two hours and 10 minutes it took us to hike the five-miles to Siler Bald and back:

- Al mentioned our mutual friend Sarah Lowell has *run* these same five miles in an hour. (Sarah is a talented and experienced trail runner; Al and I are not. Ironically today the Western States Endurance Run—a 100-mile run through the Sierra Nevada mountain range was this weekend. Al and I ran it in 2004 and 2006. Notice I say 'ran' it; that doesn't necessarily mean we finished. If you're interested in finding out how we did, you can read about it in my first book *Running through My Mind*. Cliff hang much?)

- In the early 1990's future Atlanta Centennial Park bomber Eric Rudolph was Al's 'neighbor' as he survived off the land for five years in the valley immediately below Al's cabin. In fact when the authorities captured him after the 1996 Olympics he was rummaging for food in a dumpster in nearby Murphy, North Carolina.

- Al told me I was now a 'multi-summit bagger,' meaning I had climbed to the top of two mountains. I laughed to myself as I thought back to a time several years ago when I met someone who told me he was not only a runner but a 'multi-marathoner' as well. I asked him how many marathons he had run and he proudly replied 'two.' (My point: Al has made it to the top of a couple hundred summits and I have run a couple hundred marathons, much more deserving of a 'multi' label than simply 'two.' *That's* why Al's comment struck me as funny.)

- *A Walk in the Woods,* a film starring Robert Redford and Nick Nolte and adapted from a book by Bill Bryson is being filmed in various spots along the Appalachian Trail to include the area we were in today. While we didn't spot either of the actors, we're pretty sure we stumbled across something Nick Nolte may have left behind (*if you know what I mean*). *A Walk in the Woods* is about Bryson's quest to hike the *2,181 miles of the Appalachian Trail (*the actual distance of the route according to the Appalachian Trail Conservatory).

After we finished we went back to Al's cabin to clean up before heading out to lunch Al's usual post-hike lunch spot, the Nantahala Outdoor Center. We both ordered Al's favorite, a vegan burger and I'll have to admit: After covering over 11 miles of mountain terrain I was famished; I tore into that plate of food like I hadn't eaten in days.

In fact there's a pretty good chance I may have eaten a napkin.

CHAPTER 33

Be like Mean Joe Greene

———— ∞ ————

Run my 36th consecutive Peachtree Road Race

I moved to the Atlanta area in 1979. In over 35 years the latest I ever slept in on the 4th of July was that very first year: I slept until 5:00 a.m. so I could make it to the north side of Atlanta from my home in Rex for the start of the Peachtree Road Race, a 10-kilometer run through the heart of Atlanta. Back then the race had a field of less than 10,000 runners and it wasn't hard to find a parking place in Lenox Square, a mere 60-second walk to the starting line on Peachtree Street.

This morning the routine was a little different. I woke up to a 3:45 alarm so I could drink a couple cups of coffee to get the cobwebs out and loosen up (both inside and out) before getting in the car at 5:00 and heading north on I-85. As has been my custom for the past several years, I took the exit that would take me to Piedmont Park—the coveted finish line where I would park the car and run to the starting line (to loosen up even *more*, both inside and out). This year the congestion—even at 5:45 in the morning--was a little too much for my liking. There were a lot more detours than normal on the way to the parking lot, compounded by a policeman at every intersection to complicate matters even more. On one side-street there was a policeman in a bright yellow vest spinning out of control, gesticulating wildly with his arms and shining his flashlight every which way that distracted me so much I drove straight through a stop sign. It was darn nice of him to point out my little indiscretion:

Officer Cuisinart: *'Did you see that stop sign you just went through?'*

Me (out loud): *'I was so focused on watching you giving me hand signals that I totally missed it. I'm sorry.'* (My thought balloon AKA the unfiltered version: *'Apparently not, Einstein.'*)

Officer Cuisinart: *'Get out of my sight.'*

By 6 a.m. I had the car safely parked about a half-mile from the finish line and begin my five-mile warm up run to the start. As I ran I thought about the days of Peachtree's past:

- The first one 35 years ago (only my 4th 10K ever and my first one in the state of Georgia) that I ran in 42:03 *(OK, I didn't really remember the time; I had to look it up. As I said, it was 35 years ago.).* Back then the finish was in the heart of Piedmont Park, and the common misperception for runners back then was that once they were inside the park it was time to sprint to the finish—even though there was still more than a mile remaining (a bit too long for a sprint and yes, I made that mistake more than once).

- Consistent 37- and 38-minute finishes when I was in my 30's, and holding steady in the 38-minute window into my 40's and earning a spot on the Atlanta Track Club Men's Masters (for runners 40 years and older) Competitive Team for a decade. I'll never forget the days of being in the seeded corral at the start and rubbing elbows with the human rockets from Kenya and all of the other countries where the children wear T-shirts with 'Oh, so you run a mile in under five minutes: How cute!' printed on them. While I had no legitimate business being in the seeded corral (it was easier for a masters runner to qualify for the seeded corral than it was for runners 39 and younger; after all age has *some* privileges) I really enjoyed having volunteers bringing *me* water and wet towels as I stood on Peachtree Street waiting for the race to start.

- 1996, that magical year when it was 63 degrees at the start of the race (it's not unusual for it to be in the mid-70's with 105%--*no, not a misprint*—humidity for the 7:30 a.m. start) and I ran my Peachtree best: 36:56.

- 2004, the year the wheels fell off. I ran Peachtree a mere seven days after putting my legs through 18 hours of severe torture, punishment and anguish running, walking and crawling the first 62 miles of the Western States Endurance Run and convincing the medical staff it wasn't a good idea to amputate my right leg like they wanted to do. I ran Peachtree in a (then) personal worst 45:44 and realized on that day my wheels were indeed starting to fall off. Hmmm…maybe that medical staff had the right idea after all.

- 2005, the year Peachtree turned into a 'beer run.' My goal was to drink as many free beers as I could beg, borrow and/or steal along Peachtree Street. I consumed a 'personal best' of five beers before I reached the finish line. (In the 1990's I rode a bus to Peachtree with the local running club, and after the race everyone hung out in Piedmont Park until all of the members had finished. Back then I was drinking five beers just to rehydrate.)

- 2007, the year Susan Lance and I started at the very back of the race just to see what it was like. How was it? Let's just say it won't happen again. However, I will tell you we didn't cross the starting line until 9 a.m. (the official race begins at 7:30) and that our official (run) time was just a couple of seconds more than an hour… and that with all the darting and weaving Susan and I had to do to maneuver around slower runners we probably ran a little over eight miles.

Back to today's race:

Whatever changes for the worse there were at the finish area (surely you haven't forgotten Officer Cuisinart), there were noticeable changes for the better at the starting area. There were no lines at the porta-johns (unheard of, even back in the days when Peachtree featured 'the world's longest urinal'—a metal contraption about 50 yards long that allowed 100 or more runners the option of 'no waiting' if all they needed to do was #1). The walk to the starting corral was a breeze (compared to the past couple of years when that same walk was akin to being in the crowd outside of Wal-Mart when they open their doors on Black Friday). Even the volunteers seemed more pleasant and accommodating than usual, although its entirely possible the volunteers have always been that way but I noticed it this year because on the way to the start I saw a lot of runners I've known for a very long time and for the most part they looked a lot older than they used to; gee, I wonder what happened to *them?!*

As I waited for the race to start the announcer mentioned that Meb Keflezighi, this year's Boston Marathon winner was at 'the back of the pack' with the intention of passing something like half of the runners in the field for a fundraiser. I couldn't help but think Susan Lance and I did the exact same thing seven years ago, except that no one donated any money to charity for us to do it. We just did it *because.*

Once the starter said 'go' almost two minutes passed before I actually crossed the starting line. I started out at a conservative pace, a pace that allowed me to notice free beer on my left from a Mexican restaurant about one mile into the race and two miles later free beer from a local tavern on my right. As I wanted to get a 'Time Group A' seeding next year (requiring a finish of less than 48 minutes) I couldn't afford the time to belly up to the bar as I had done during my 'beer run' days.

As I made my way up Heartbreak Hill (about three miles into the run) I noticed the medical offices of the neurosurgeon who recommended I take up yoga as a way of 'curing the ills of Western States' in my right leg. When I saw him 10 months ago he asked me to touch my toes. Laughing, I barely touched the middle of my shins. Today I can touch the back of my middle knuckle to the floor. In about three more miles I'll have a gauge to see if the yoga is helping my running. (Last year's Peachtree time? 50:24. Make a mental note: You'll need this later.)

Heading up the second hill—and in my opinion the more difficult of the two, this one leading up to Colony Square I noticed two healthy looking men in their 20's stopping to walk and catch their breath. I couldn't help but feel proud of myself for keeping the same pace I had been running for four-and-a-half miles…when a young boy who couldn't have been more than 12 years old pulled up alongside me and asked me how far we still had to run. 'About a mile-and-a-half,' I told him. Well, actually all he heard was 'about-a-mile' because he never heard the 'and-a-half' part because he was 50 yards in front of me before I could get the words out of my mouth.

As I made the final left hand turn to the final downhill leading to the finish line I felt good about my chances of finishing in less than 48 minutes. If I don't trip over any speed bumps, street reflectors or discarded beer cans I should make it with a few seconds to spare.

Thirty-eight. That's the number of seconds I had to spare. I crossed the finish line with 47:22 (actually 47:21:89) showing on my chronograph. It's official: I'll be in Time Group 'A' when I line up for my 37th Peachtree Road Race, my first at the age of 60. (Note: The standards for sub-seeded times haven't changed. In other words, for me to rub elbows with the Kenyans ever again I have to meet the same standards set forth for a 40-year old. Age has lost some of its privilege at Peachtree, but then again I *do* get a 5% discount on my groceries on Wednesdays. Also, the yoga appears to be working.)

Now for the moment I've been waiting for: My 'Mean Joe Greene' moment. For those of you who don't remember (or never knew to begin with) there was a famous commercial for a certain carbonated beverage (that happens to be made in Atlanta) starring Mean Joe Greene, a player on the talented Pittsburgh Steeler teams of the 1970's. After a game a young boy—about the same age as the boy who dusted me on the Colony Square hill—handed an obviously exhausted Greene his bottle of soda on his way to the locker room. Greene gulped it down and started to walk away, only to turn around and say 'hey, kid; catch' while tossing the young boy his jersey. The young boy—obviously—is overjoyed *('Hey, thanks Mean Joe!')*.

So after the race I picked up my Peachtree T-shirt (coveted in certain circles) and scoured the crowd lining the wire fence around Piedmont Park for just the right boy for my Mean Joe Greene scenario to play out. I walked a couple hundred yards and found my intended target: A boy of about 10 or 11 standing between his mom and dad with his eyes as wide as the coaster my beer is resting on at the moment. Perfect: His mom and dad aren't running so he won't be getting a Peachtree T-Shirt from them, he appeared to be excited about seeing all the runners who have just run in *the* Peachtree Road Race and in all honesty looked a lot like what I imagine my grandson will look like in another five or six years. I smiled at the boy, tossed him my shirt and said 'hey, kid; catch' albeit not in the same deep, raspy voice of Mean Joe Greene. I walked a few steps, smiling at myself at the possibility of making someone's day when I heard someone running up behind me and grabbing my left arm.

'Hey mister, this isn't my size. Have you got one in a small?'

CHAPTER 34

Fartleks with the Fox

———— ✺ ————

Outfox a Fox

Running early in the morning has its advantages. It offers solitude, peace of mind and the opportunity to engage in nature that otherwise would be difficult once the sun comes up and the world springs to life. But early in the morning—roughly a couple of hours before the roosters crow in a brand new day—there isn't much of a chance to run into any other human beings. However, having lived in the same house for the past two dozen years and running the same three or four routes every morning during that time, I've gotten to know some of the local denizens on a first name basis. Granted they don't know my name—mainly because they're either deer, possums, raccoons, rabbits, squirrels or armadillos—but I certainly know theirs. I also know where they live, when there are new additions to their families (or sadly, on occasion, losses) and how adept they are at crossing the road when the occasional vehicle poses a threat.

Another advantage for me personally is that I have little traffic to contend with at that time of day (night?). Sure there have been exceptions over the years such as:

- An afternoon run in the early 1980's in Rex, Georgia when a country boy drove past me in one of those trucks with tires better suited for a passenger aircraft decided my head was the perfect target for his beer bottle throwing practice (he missed, thankfully).

- The occasional joker who drives towards me at 55 miles an hour and considers 'let's see how fast the runner jumps up on the curb when I veer towards him' a great way to start the day.

- On the mornings—always Saturdays or Sundays—I run at 2 a.m. because the rest of my day will be spent volunteering at a race and encounter the occasional 'drive by' who is actually at the tail end of *their* Friday or Saturday *night* and gets a lot of joy out of harassing someone out for some exercise before their alcohol-induced buzz wears off.

But these are truly the exceptions; for the most part I feel very safe during my morning runs. I always take a flashlight with me, wear reflective shoes and clothing and steer clear of headphones. Finally, if there's one thing I've learned over the years it's how to steer clear of oncoming vehicles. I doubt I'd be writing this if I weren't.

But this morning was different. I didn't feel safe. Not by a long shot.

Before I get to the details, a little background is in order.

I came face-to-face with a crazed squirrel almost half a century ago in Davisville, Rhode Island. The squirrel and I were walking towards one another on a dirt trail through the woods behind our house. Our eyes met. We both froze. Suddenly the squirrel ran towards me. I remained frozen. The squirrel clawed his way up my leg, my torso and ultimately my face. I ran home in horror. My mom took me to the emergency room within a couple of seconds where my one thousand tiny lacerations were tended to (I admit I may have exaggerated slightly; it may have been a couple of *minutes*—not seconds--before I got to the emergency room. What do I know; I was in shock.).

So ever since that day I have a distrust of squirrels. Not necessarily a *fear* of squirrels, mind you; I just don't trust the little bastards.

Continuing with more background:

At the beginning of three of the last four spring seasons a family of foxes has taken residence under the utility shed in our back yard. The first year we noticed them I called animal control to ask for guidance. I was told there was nothing they could do in the way of capturing them and releasing them into the wild, but they did tell me I could hire someone to remove them from my property (in other words, I could call 'The Terminator'). I wasn't about to cause any harm to the little guys because, quite frankly it was one of the highlights of our evenings when the cubs (baby foxes) came out from under the shed around dusk and frolicked in the back yard like a bunch of newborn puppies. Many a night Cindy and I would sit on the back porch sipping wine, watching the cubs chase one another from one end of the stacked stone wall in the back yard to the other. This year we counted a record-high number of cubs: seven.

They're gone from the back yard now (they usually only stick around for a couple of weeks), but there are other foxes along my regular running routes that I know on the aforementioned first name basis. One of them *(Oscar, named after the character on Sesame Street who lives in a trashcan because this particular fox always runs behind a trashcan when he sees me. Yes, it's a male fox; don't ask me how I know—I just do)* crosses my path about once every 10 days about a mile from my house in the vicinity of a streetlight. This morning I saw Oscar, who in turn saw me and headed towards his trash can...only to turn around and start walking towards me as I got within 50 yards of him. I stopped, he continued.

>*Time out: There have been reports of rabid foxes in the area lately. I thought you should know; that way you won't think of me as a chicken sh*t as you read on.*

I thought to myself that no one deserves to be bit by a rabid fox at 5 a.m. on a Thursday morning so I started running as fast as my legs would take me. Oscar fell in behind, matching me stride-for-stride.

Time out: Peachtree City is notorious for its lack of artificial lighting. Sure, there are streetlights—one of them happens to be Oscar's favorite hangout—but they're spread pretty far apart along the roads.

I turned back and shined my flashlight in the middle of the street to see how close Oscar was. I saw two specks of light very close to one another: They could be Oscar's eyes and then again they could be the reflectors in the center of the street illuminated by my flashlight. Not having the time to determine exactly *what* they were, I had to assume the two lights were indeed Oscar and ran as fast as I possibly could to the next streetlight, where I would once again have the opportunity to gauge how close Oscar was and whether or not I might be spending the morning in the emergency room.

Time out: A fartlek is a workout comprised of running at various speeds for varying distances. For example a workout might consist of a slow, easy jog with the occasional all-out sprint thrown in from, say 'the fire hydrant on the right to three mailboxes down on the left.'

I stopped beneath the safe zone of the light beneath the streetlight and looked back in horror to see Oscar emerging from the pitch black of the shaded road into the illuminated clearing where I had stopped to assess the situation. I did just that (assessed the situation) and I can tell you one thing: It wasn't pretty: There simply wasn't any 'quit' in Oscar.

The fartleks continued for two more streetlights—Oscar still in what I would call 'casual pursuit'—until a car sped towards me, providing me the opportunity to escape whatever horror Oscar hoped to reign down on me. Immediately after the car passed me and was positioned between Oscar and I, I ducked into the woods and ran a circuitous route back to my house with the hope that Oscar would continue down the road. I won't say that the plan worked exactly as planned, but I will say that when I got to my front porch and surveyed the front yard and the street running in front of my house there wasn't a trace of Oscar.

> *Final time out: Escaping the jaws of Oscar the Fox was quite
> a relief. I felt like the Roadrunner in the cartoons who always
> managed to elude the evil clutches of Wile E. Coyote.*

> *Final time out (this time I mean it): A roadrunner's top speed is about
> 20 miles per hour, while coyotes can reach speeds up to 43 miles per hour.
> My bowling team in college (The Acme Bowling Team, named after the
> company from which Wile E. Coyote always ordered the contraptions he
> used to try and catch the roadrunner) sported a patch on our shirtsleeves
> with Wile E. Coyote grabbing the Roadrunner by the throat.*

So to you, Oscar the Fox I leave you with the embroidered caption on
that patch:

> *Beep Beep My A**!*

CHAPTER 35

My Mister Magoo Moment

━━━━━━━━━━━━━━ ⚬❀❀⚬ ━━━━━━━━━━━━━━

Admit to myself: I'm getting older

My wife and I have been playing music trivia with a group of friends once a week for the past eight years. We're known as the Fried Mushrooms—'FM' for short'—and we've gotten to be quite competitive over the years. For most of the members of our team, 'competitive' means we pretty much know our stuff.

But I'm not 'most members.' To me 'competitive' means exactly what it implies: An aversion to losing. Losing sucks, otherwise it wouldn't be called losing. Just win, baby.

Now hold onto that thought because I'm about to tell you why tonight sucked. And it wasn't because we didn't know our stuff. Not even close.

Let me first explain the format for the music trivia competition: The official **Rules of Engagement:**

- There are four rounds consisting of four songs each.

- Each round has a 'theme.'

- Three points each are awarded for correctly identifying the song title, the artist and the year of release (plus or minus one year) and if all three are correctly answered there is a bonus of one point.

- There is also a halftime trivia question (worth 10 points and based on 'Today in Music History') and a final 'Jeopardy-style' question where you can wager at least one and up to all of your points.

- Prizes are awarded for first, second* (or 'first loser,' as I call it) and third (or 'third' as the rest of my team calls it).

*If you don't think finishing in second place sucks,
ask any player on the losing team
in the Super Bowl how they feel after the big game.*

Tonight's competition was a little different: Five bonus points would be awarded if the year was identified exactly. Do you know what happens when the reward is magnified? It has the same effect on my competitive nature.

The first round was my worst nightmare: Classic Country. If I were to play music trivia by myself, my team name would be 'No Country for Old Man' because in all honesty, I hate that sh*t. Let me rephrase it another way: I hate that sh*t. (Sorry, I tried.) However, tonight's country music round was different than normal: I actually knew some of the songs. *A Boy Named Sue* (Johnny Cash, 1969), *The Most Beautiful Girl in the World* (Charlie Rich, 1973) and *Mountain Music* (Alabama, 1982); yep, nailed them all. Even the fourth song I was able to correctly name the title (I guess listening to the song paid off): *Silver Wings*. Here's the strangest part: If I were playing as 'No Country for Old Man' against the country experts on the Fried Mushrooms I would have been ahead of them after the first round. Yes sir; I was *el fuego*.

The second round was right up my alley: Obscure Hits of the '60's and '70's. *Season of the Witch* (the Donovan version, not the Vanilla Fudge remake), *Mississippi Queen*, *Moondance* and *Rock and Roll Hoochie Koo*. With the exception of *Moondance* (The year of release was 1970; I said

1977 because that's what displays on the '70's channel every time it plays. Thanks for nothing, XM radio.) we had a perfect round and took a commanding lead into halftime, especially after answering the halftime question correctly (something about a roadie for Def Leppard losing his life prior to a 1988 concert).

Halftime is a 10-minute break in the action after the second round that I normally use to eat my dinner that has been sitting in front of me for anywhere from five to 30 minutes, depending on what I order, how busy the restaurant is and whether or not a country music round was played in the second round because if that's the case I can spend the second round eating since I never have anything to contribute because I don't know sh*t about country music. Except tonight, because I was *el fuego*.

Speaking of being on fire, tonight was the first time I ordered the hottest chicken wing in the restaurant: Venom. I asked the waitress if that meant they were 'flavor hot' or 'hot-for-the-sake-of-being-hot hot.' She said the former; it was the latter. How did I feel after eating a single chicken wing? Imagine coating your lips with a layer of lighter fluid—how are you doing so far?—and then pressing your lips against a lit match. Like I said: *El fuego*.

The third round was sort of up my alley: One Hit Wonders of VH1. *Tarzan Boy* (Baltimora, 1986—I missed this the first two times I ever heard it and I SWORE I would never miss it again. So far so good.), *99 Luftballoons* (Nena, 1984), *Funky Town* (Lipps Inc., 1980) and *Hooked on a Feeling* (Blue Swede, 1974—at first I wasn't sure if I was making up the name of the group or if it was buried in the deep recesses of my mind. Fortunately it was the latter.).

With a huge lead going into **the fourth round** it was virtually impossible for us to reach the final Jeopardy-style question without being in first place. That was a good thing for us because the fourth round was '90's R & B.' Remember how bad I said I was at country music? Our *entire team* is that bad at '90's R & B. And boy did it show tonight. We only named one song correctly (only because the singer said 'This is how we do it' over and over and over again) and two years of release correctly (we guessed on both of them). As for the artists, I'm pretty sure we were making some of them up and no--Blue Swede was not one of them.

The final question calls for a wager with only one stipulation: You have to bet at least one point. In spite of our horrendous fourth round we were still in first place. Comfortably. The category—released on Facebook earlier in the day--for the final question was 'Current Weird Al.' An internet search revealed Weird Al Yankovic had just released a new album and a new song was being released on video for eight consecutive days. Today happened to be the third day.

I meticulously looked over the point totals for each team. As we often do when we have the lead at the end of the fourth round, we wagered just enough points to beat the second-place team by one point should we both answer the question correctly and the second-place team bet all of its points. I double- and triple-checked my math and when I was comfortable with my calculation I turned in our wager.

The final question asked for the names of the first three songs Weird Al had released. We answered correctly, as did the second-place team. As the host of the event always does, he read off the name of the third-place team first. Next he read the name of the second-place (first loser) team: *Fried Mushrooms*. Finally, in first place was the team I wagered enough points to beat by one point should we both answer the question correctly, which we did.

Second place? Not according to my math. On two occasions over the years I've challenged our announced point totals when I thought the DJ made a mistake. I was right on both occasions and I was all about to go *el fuego* on his a** when I realized the mistake was not his, but mine.

You see, our total points after four rounds was 142. Without my reading glasses on my '2' looked an awful lot like an '8' and I had based our final wager on our team having 148 points; not 142.

Hey everybody, look! Mister Magoo is playing music trivia tonight!

Tonight it would have helped if I had applied the 'four eyes' principle to my wager and had someone else on the team double check my math. Or at the very least my penmanship.

Next week I assure you I won't make the same mistake, because next week the 'four eyes' will be all mine: I'll be wearing my reading glasses.

That way I'll know the score... as well as be able to read the menu so I'm not at the mercy of the waitress to offer culinary suggestions that make my mouth *el fuego*.

CHAPTER 36

Moving Violations

―――――∞∞∞――――――

Move to the Country

My family moved around quite a bit while I was growing up. Of course that was all part of being raised in a military household as every Army, Navy, Air Force and Marine brat can attest to.

I was born in Virginia, where my dad—a career Navy man was stationed at the time. As a youngster I spent a little time in Pennsylvania as well during the summer months and occasionally when my dad was away at sea. Both of my parents' families lived in the small town of Birdsboro; I can still remember it feeling like Christmas every time I had the opportunity to spend time with two sets of grandparents as well as a full complement of aunts, uncles and cousins.

The first time the U.S. Navy asked our family to move they didn't pull any punches. Destination: Den Hague, the Netherlands. From that point on every three years the Ludwig family would be asked to move to (in order) Quonset Point, Rhode Island; Pearl Harbor, Hawaii; and Mayport, Florida. The point I'm trying to make is that for the first 18 years of my life moving from one home to another was not a matter of choice, but rather where the U.S. Navy wanted us to be at that particular point in time.

Attending the University of Florida after high school was a matter of choice. During my tenure in Gainesville I lived (in order) in a non-air conditioned dormitory, a fraternity house (I slept in a loft about the size of a double-wide coffin), a trailer (single-wide) and an apartment in an off-campus married housing complex. From my perspective all of them were not a matter of choice but rather a matter of necessity, if not downright affordability.

After graduation I relocated to Atlanta in search of a job. I rented an apartment and was fortunate to find employment with a company located barely a mile from my front door. Within a year Cindy and I bought our first house in Rex, Georgia. I would love to be able to tell you it was our dream home but in all honesty it was merely a comfortable split-foyer house we could afford that wasn't located too far away from either of our jobs. Ten years later we moved to our next house in Peachtree City, Georgia. It was a nice house but again, it was simply one we could afford and didn't add too much to our daily commutes. We figured it was a small price to pay for the education our two sons would receive in the reputable Fayette County School System.

So after calling a dozen places 'home' for a variety of reasons (because the U.S. Navy said so, because of economic considerations, for the welfare of our children) we were ready to find a house that we could truly call 'home.' A house we wanted to live in for one reason and one reason only: It was the house *we* wanted to call 'home.' After looking at an assortment of houses in Senoia, Georgia for the better part of two years we finally found what we were looking for: A place with the potential to be the first, and perhaps last place we call 'home.'

But this story isn't about that. Rather this story is about the misery of moving the accumulation of 24 years living under one roof from one house to another. My initial thought of *'it's only 10 miles away—how hard can it be?'* proved to be the dumbest idea since automobile manufacturers stopped putting the gas cap behind license plates where they belong and began putting them on both sides of the car so now when you stop for fuel you're forced to play a game of 'gas station musical chairs' because half of the cars are trying to align themselves on the right side of the gas pump and the other half on the left resulting in the biggest cluster F this side of a Black Friday sale at Walmart. But I digress, because this story isn't about that either.

'How hard can it be?'

Let me preface this by saying I thought moving the small stuff and having a moving company move the big stuff would make the transition from one house to another fairly simple. After all we had almost two months to complete the entire move, set up the house in Senoia and make the Peachtree City house available to rent.

'How hard can it be?' I'll tell you how hard it can be: The neighbors started calling me 'Chief Brody' because they perceived the contents of my house as being a Great White shark eating me alive just as the shark wanted to do to the protagonist in Peter Benchley's *Jaws*.

Here's how the move from one house to another devoured me one bite at a time:

- How did packing the smaller items and taking them to the new house one 2004 Nissan Frontier truckload at a time work out? Imagine one of the Great Lakes dried up and you've been tasked with filling it back up with water using only a two-gallon bucket and a faucet located 10 miles away from the shore. And coincidentally the bucket has a small leak. Not a very pretty picture, is it?

- I was packing up my CD's—in alphabetical order, of course—when my older son came over to help me load the truck. Apparently he thought 'load the truck' meant 'see if there are any CD's you don't want so they don't need to be taken to the new house 'cuz I'll be glad to take them off your hands.' Damn generation gap.

- After two weeks of taking a daily truckload of small boxes to the new house I decided to rent a ten-foot truck to speed things up and get everything I could over there before the movers came to get the big stuff. The rental company only had a 24-foot truck available but for only $10 more than a 10-footer I thought for that price it wouldn't be a big deal if half of the truck was empty. Suffice it to say I used every cubic inch of that 24-footer. Apparently judging the cumulative size of a bunch of CD's, dinnerware and assorted shoes, socks and underwear stuffed inside of black garbage bags is not my forte.

- I consulted with a moving company over the phone and provided them an itemized list of what I wanted them to move. I was told the move would require one 40-foot truckload and between three and four hours for the entire process of loading, transporting and unloading those items. Two full truckloads, two trips to the new house and nine-and-a-half hours later the move was complete. Apparently the moving company is worse at this game than I am.

- One of the young men working for the moving company came to Cindy and I and said *'I've got to be honest; I bumped the corner of this headboard against the wall on the way up the stairs. There's no major damage; just a little bump on the corner here.'* It brought to mind the scene in *Monty Python and the Holy Grail* when the Black Knight loses both arms in a sword fight and says 'it's only a flesh wound.'

- My grandson helped me pack some of the remaining items in the old house. I loaded about three dozen cartons while he called it quits after finding his long-lost foam rubber sword. Two hours later as we were driving to the new house he had this to say: *'When we get to the new house you unload the boxes and I'll take a bath.'* Less than 25 minutes later he was in the tub splashing his foam rubber sword while I was unloading about three dozen cartons.

- During the four-week process of packing and moving I always had an ample supply of cold bottled water available for whoever may be helping (or bathing). Seeing as the move was made in July in the hot and humid Deep South, a fresh supply of water never lasted very long. Conservatively I bought enough bottled water to raise the water level of Lake Erie 18 inches.

- My grandson was with me when the interior of the old house was being painted. I gave him one rule to follow: *Don't touch the walls!* I asked him a good two dozen times throughout the afternoon what is the ONE rule and each time without hesitation he said 'don't touch the walls.' As we were getting ready to leave I asked him if he touched any walls. *'No, G-Pa, I didn't touch any walls.'* Of course then I had to ask him why there was a tiny beige handprint on the front of his black shirt.

- I've called my grandson 'Tiger' ever since he learned to speak. One particularly trying day while I was doing about six things at once between the two houses (moving furniture into the new house, doing yard work at the old house and making sure my grandson didn't touch any wet paint, to name a few) my grandson asked to do something straight out of left field (go to a movie, build a rocket ship) and I said: 'You know I'm doing all these things so now isn't a good time.' His reply: *'But I'm your Tiger!'* F. Lee Bailey couldn't have presented a more compelling or convincing argument.

Now that the move is over, the old house is rented and the new house is starting to come together I'd like to tell you I can look back and laugh at the thought I originally had of 'how hard could it be.'

I'd like to, but if I did I'd be lying.

The move from Peachtree City to Senoia proved to be more difficult than filling up with gas at a Quick Trip at 5:00 on a Friday afternoon in the midst of a battle of Gas Cap Roulette.

Indoctrination to Country Living

After living in the country for a month or so, Cindy and I have been through Round One of our Indoctrination to Country Living. I'm here to tell you: It's been an education. Here's what we've learned so far.

- Cell phone service is marginal at best. I have to drive two miles from home to get a signal. We're virtually living in Cell Phone Hell. But you get used to it; as a matter of fact I'm beginning to enjoy the solitude that only being unreachable by cell phone can bring. Sure, there's the landline, but the only calls I get on it are the ones from marketers and solicitors. Of course there is one other way I can be reached…

- That would be via the Internet. When there is a connection, that is. When we had our Internet connected there was only one problem: It didn't get connected. I asked my IT guy at work to take a look at it. One day at the office I gave him the house key so he could drop by and take a look. 'It will be easy,' he said. 'I won't be there when you get home.' One hour later he called: 'Can you meet me at Best Buy? We're going to need a new modem.' Two hours and $100 later, the new modem is connected. As for the connection to the Internet? Not so much. A few days later a technician from our service provider showed up at the house. 'Piece of cake,' he said. He walked into the office where the computer sat on my desk, looked at the modem and screamed '*What's that?*' with the same emotion you and I would have if we saw a rat with a human head. It would be another six weeks before we finally had resolution and a connection to the Internet, no thanks to our service provider.

- There's a woman who lives off Highway 16—about a quarter mile east of Highway 54—who has a 'Barbie Beach' in her front yard. It's exactly what you think it is: A small patch of sand carved out in the middle of the grass where you'll find a host of Barbie dolls in different attire, poses and décor in support of any number of topical themes. Halloween, football season and summertime are three that immediately come to mind. There's a hand-scribbled sign (I say 'scribbled' because it looks like it was written by finger... in blood) in the front yard indicating where one should park their vehicle to visit Barbie Beach. I've never stopped because I fear if I did the next time anyone saw me I would be a lampshade.

- I've learned a thing or two about armadillos. They're blind as bats, they dig like gophers, they're slow as possums and they appear to be part shellfish. When you startle them in the morning and they take off running on the road they sound like a bowling ball rolling across your driveway. Also, they are BUTT UGLY, if said butt was covered with wrinkles and an armor plate.

- There are a lot of trucks in the country, many of them with those really big tires that make a step stool a necessity for climbing into the cab. The drivers seem to enjoy trying to force me off the side of the road when I'm running. Silly country folk: They don't know I went to the University of Florida where a course in dodging traffic is part of the required core curriculum.

- Speaking of driving on the country roads, I've learned that speed limits are nothing more than suggestions. I drive to work early in the morning—well before sunrise—and tend to take it easy just in case I have to dodge any deer along the way. *(The Three D's of Country Driving: Dark + Deer = Death.)* So the signs suggesting I drive 55 miles per hour are pushing my oh-dark-thirty limit. Those big-wheeled trucks I mentioned earlier? They are literally crawling up my a** in the morning, alternating between flashing their bright lights in my rear view mirror and veering to the left of the solid yellow stripe to see if they have enough time to speed up and get in front of me. I have yet to see any flashing blue lights in the morning, but with my luck when I do it will be to redirect traffic while I'm trying to remove a deer from the front grill of my car.

- Speaking of flashing blue lights, I understand it's considered felonious to have the front tires of your vehicle touching or—God forbid—protruding past the solid white line at a red light and a crime punishable by you-don't-wanna-know for rolling through a stop sign. Sorry Dorothy, you're not in Mayberry anymore.

Today we have cell phone service—thanks to a tower. We have a connection to the Internet. I rarely answer the landline, so if you called me and I didn't answer I apologize. (I'm totally lying; I hate answering the phone when I'm at home. Yes, even for you.) I haven't gotten any tickets from the men in blue. I have, however bagged one deer (so far). I've dodged every single truck with those 'over compensated' tires I was telling you about. I've outrun dozens of armadillos during my morning runs.

And I haven't been made into a lampshade.

So far.

CHAPTER 37

Put a Fork in It

❦

Dine at Abdullah's

Having the urge to do something dangerous—something that would put my life on the line—I considered hang gliding, rappelling and climbing Mount Everest. With my extreme fear of heights firmly in mind I opted to try something that would keep my feet on the ground and close to home instead. Eating at Abdullah the Butcher's House of Ribs and Chinese Food fit the bill: It was right around the corner from my place of employment, it allowed the possibility of meeting 'The Madman from Sudan' (as Abdullah was known in the world of professional wrestling) and the whole idea was a lot more exciting and living-on-the-edge than my usual weekday lunch consisting of a turkey sandwich, chips and a Little Debbie cake.

A little background about Abdullah is in order first. Larry Shreve—'Abdullah'—was born in Canada back in 1941. He had a long and notorious career as a 'heel' (bad guy) in professional wrestling and his signature move was grabbing his opponent in a headlock, removing a fork he had concealed in his wrestling trunks and jamming it into his opponent's forehead (drawing a considerable amount of the red stuff, of course). Remember: This is back when wrestling was *real* (pre-Vince McMahon).

So four of my co-workers and I piled into my car and headed out for Abdullah's. One brought a fork along with him—just in case there was the opportunity to pose for a Facebook-worthy photo with Mr. Madman. As I was driving another of my co-workers gave me a tour: 'This is where the chop shop used to be…this is where the strip club used to be…' I began feeling silly for worrying what I would soon be eating; hell, tainted food was merely a blip on the radar at this point.

On an August afternoon with temperatures in the mid-90's we were looking forward to getting inside the restaurant where we would be met with…temperatures in the low 100's! Apparently pink brick buildings don't take kindly to a hot summer sun, particularly pink brick buildings with no air conditioning. The ceiling fans were at full strength, presumably to keep the steam in the air hovering near the ground and well below knee level. Now that the stage has been set, let's move on to the food.

The prepared food was displayed in (I'll call them) troughs housed in glass. If I didn't know better I could have easily mistaken the food (ox neck?) as props used in the 'Toxic Avenger' movies of the 1980's. Not familiar with the movies? Imagine this formula: *The Walking Dead* + a lot more gore – every iota of plot = *Toxic Avenger*. I ordered from the Chinese portion of the menu because (a) none of it was in the troughs in the front and (b) I was told it was 'prepared fresh' in the back. It also meant everyone else in my party would be finished eating their lunch before mine was even ready (although I managed to eat a couple bites of my sesame chicken and rice before we got up from the table…and I did have plenty left over for lunch the next day).

The clientele? Hard to say, because on this day the clientele consisted of our party of five (sans the one or two men who came in to pick up their order which they probably ate on one of the tables outside where it was 10 or so degrees cooler than it was inside).

So let me play 'food critic' for a moment. Ambiance: Think high school locker room. Food: Quite honestly mine was pretty good; the others in my party who ate 'trough food' were satisfied with theirs as well. Price:

Let me just say it's hard to put a dollar value on your life. Clientele: Since it was only us…

Having grown up in the era of REAL professional wrestling, as we were leaving I had to stop to look at some of the photos on the wall. Let me correct that: I had to stop to look at ALL of the photos on ALL four walls. It was like going back in time: Superstar Billy Graham…Kamala, the Ugandan Warrior…Coco B. Ware…Moon Dog Spot…Ricky 'the Dragon' Steamboat…Hulk Hogan…Dusty Rhodes…Jimmy 'Superfly' Snuka… Black Jack Mulligan…the Rock and Roll Express…

It seems like I saw the battle scarred faces of virtually every wrestler I grew up with during those 15 minutes. Everyone except one, that is.

We didn't get to meet Mr. Abdullah the Butcher: Wrestler, restaurateur and Madman from Sudan.

My friend never even got to take his fork out of his pocket; presumably because he ordered from the trough and ate his lunch through a straw.

CHAPTER 38

Take Me Out of the Ball Game

—∞∞∞—

Attend an American vs. National League Baseball Game

I put myself on a self-imposed four-and-a-half month moratorium on professional sports after my Florida Gators lost in the Final Four last April, deciding to wait for the first hint of fall when college football was back in session before I gave ESPN another thought. It wasn't too difficult, seeing as I swore 20 years ago I would never contribute another cent to the NFL, the NBA, the PGA, the NHL or Major League Baseball following the latter's strike in 1994. This year I decided to take it up a notch and skip watching these sports on television (essentially free) as well. I can think of lots of things I'd rather do than watch an outfielder standing around for a few hours making more money catching two or three balls and adjusting his jock strap a couple hundred times than most people make in an entire year. Off the top of my head that list would include sliding off the seat of a bicycle and landing on the center bar, drinking a pint of soured milk while eating a dish of refried beans and never again mentioning my theory of what it really means when someone smokes a cigar.

So how did I end up at Turner Field one hot August night to see the Atlanta Braves take on the Oakland Athletics? It was my company summer family outing and the tickets were complementary. Plus there was a pregame cookout and the occasion provided an opportunity to see the employees away from work and visit with their families, something I don't get to do very often but enjoy when I do. In other words, I really wasn't there to see the game. But since the game was against the A's and since I've never seen a team from the American League in person (although I was a huge Boston Red Sox fan in the mid-'60's when we lived in Rhode Island), this seemed like the right game to see. Plus I wasn't going to have to pay for it (more on that later).

I've been to the stadium where the Braves play many times. The Atlanta Marathon (my favorite race) used to start and finish there. Lots of 5K and 10K races, charity walks and athletic events have been held there. I've even been to a dozen or more Braves games (pre-1994, of course). But I can honestly say that this last trip to the stadium will in all likelihood be my last. The Atlanta Marathon is no more; I don't run many 5 and 10K's and the Braves are moving to Gwinnett County in a few years. The stadium is scheduled for demolition: What a waste; the stadium was originally built to host the 1996 Olympics in Atlanta and for all intents and purposes is still very modern and in reasonably good shape (if you don't factor in the horrific parking facilities; more on that later as well).

Cindy and I invited our good friends Chuck and Jan to the game. Chuck is a huge Braves fan and I knew that unless the score of the game was 100 to nothing after a couple of innings—in the A's favor, of course--there was no chance in hell of us leaving early and beating the mass exodus out of the confusing parking lots after the game was over. With my bad luck I expected we'd be in for a pitcher's duel--baseball's interpretation of a soccer game--that would essentially guarantee we'd be in our seats until the very last out was made.

As I heard the announcement of the starting lineup I didn't recognize the name of any player on the A's, although when I heard the name 'Coco Crisp' it sounded slightly familiar until I realized I was probably thinking about the name of a cereal rather than a center fielder. After all it's been a long time since I was a fan of the A's back when Charlie Finley was the owner, handlebar mustaches were rampant in their dugout and zealous A's fans wore baseball caps with 'F___in' A's embroidered on them (Note: The

A's won three straight World Series in the early '70's so yeah, they were indeed the F___in' A's).

I recognized a couple of names on the Braves and thought it sounded kind of odd when they announced the manager's name and it wasn't Bobby Cox. I believe it was Freddy something-or-other (Mercury? Krueger? Sorry; wasn't listening/don't care).

Although we had pretty good seats (it was 7 p.m. in August so any seats in the shade are considered 'pretty good'), I wondered why I wasn't sitting in the owner's box. After all, my teller friend at the bank is married to the man who is the brother of the General Manager of the Braves and in a Major-League-Baseball-Six-Degrees-of-Kevin-Bacon kind of way, I considered myself practically a part of the team.

The game had its fair share of highs and lows, the biggest high being that the Braves were ahead from the moment they scored two runs in the bottom of the first until their star closer Craig 'Unleash the' Kimbrel finished off the A's in the top of the ninth and preserved a 4-3 victory. A quick note to the Braves front office: At the beginning of the ninth inning my ears started bleeding the moment the organist began playing *Welcome to the Jungle*. For the love of all things holy, please ask him/her to stop. If you insist on playing the song, use the original from Guns N' Roses; they need all the hype they can get.

As for the biggest low that would be a three-way-tie between paying $4.50 for a bag of Cracker Jacks (On this night the 100-year anniversary of the 'miracle' Boston Braves winning the series was commemorated and Cracker Jacks were announced as costing only 25 cents; maybe that $4.50 was the 2014 conversion of a 1914 quarter.), spending 40 minutes in line waiting to get out of the no-architect-in-his-right-mind-would-design parking lot (Nice job flashing those neon nightsticks around, parking lot attendants with no clue about traffic control!) and watching the naked man who ran from the first base dugout into shallow center field in the sixth inning before calmly surrendering himself to the police...who promptly body-slammed him to the ground before carting him off to (I'm going out on a limb here) the owner's box (I figured they had room for one more since I wasn't sitting there-- despite my Kevin Bacon-like ties to the Braves).

I didn't leave with any souvenir baseballs of my last trip to Turner Field even though we were sitting pretty close to third base, albeit about 1,500 feet ABOVE third base. There was one foul ball that I might have had a chance catching if I had a glove. A glove on the end of my 184-foot long arm, that is. What I did leave with was an evening of entertainment that I'll remember long after the stadium closes its doors and becomes part of America's passed time, if you know what I mean (Read: Demolished).

For now just take me out of the ball game. At least until college football starts in a couple of weeks.

CHAPTER 39

Where Cell Phones go to Die

---∞∞∞---

Live in the Country

I've always lived in the city. Small yards, busy streets and neighbors a little too close for comfort. Dogs on leashes with their owners close behind, a plastic bag in hand 'just in case.' Sidewalks and side streets littered with light posts, fire hydrants and mail boxes. Cars everywhere; if not a car then a van, a motorcycle or (God forbid) an RV. People reluctant to make a quick trip to the grocery store if they don't think they can be seen in public 'like that.'

You may have gathered I'm not particularly fond of living in the city. However for almost six decades the city has for all intents and purposes been holding me hostage. Not in a gun-to-the-head-'til-the-ransom-is-paid kind of way, but rather a live-in-the-city-or-pay-the-consequences kind of way which is actually sort of the same thing so don't you worry your purty little head none (I'm already speaking country!). Eighteen years as a Navy brat living in military housing, six years of college at a major university and 35 years working for two employers that required living in the city to avoid a daily commute more suitable for a Greyhound bus than a personal vehicle never made country living a viable option.

But after more than two years of toying with the idea of moving to the country Cindy and I finally did it: We pulled the plug on city life. Cue the theme song from *Green Acres*:

'You are my wife…goodbye city life.'

If you're not familiar with the show, *Green Acres* was a comedy in the mid-to-late '60's starring Eddie Albert (aptly playing the role of a New York attorney) and his wife Eva Gabor (portraying his wife although basically playing herself, an uppity Hungarian bombshell) who gives up life in the city (his idea) to live on a farm in Hooterville, USA.

Now where was I? Oh yeah, we up and pulled the plug on city life (I did it again!) and moved to the small town of Senoia, Georgia. Better known as the base of operations for the hit television series *The Walking Dead*, Senoia is located about 35 miles south of Atlanta and has a population of…well, let's just say there are more people on a naval aircraft carrier than there are residents of Senoia. But that's not necessarily a bad thing. In my opinion it's a good thing; a *very* good thing. It's so quiet living out in the country the only sounds I hear sitting on my back porch are crickets chirping at dusk, roosters crowing at dawn and the distant sound of locomotives making their way along the tracks a fur piece down the road.

Although I'm barely three weeks removed from life in the city I've already gotten quite the how-do-you-do to living in the country:

- I got behind a tractor the other day as I was driving home from work. It was barely going 20 miles per hour on a road with a speed limit of 45. Actually I wasn't directly behind the tractor: I was behind the car behind the car behind the truck behind the car behind the tractor. No one appears to be in a hurry in Senoia. OK with me.

- I know Atlanta has a fair share of streets with 'Peachtree' in the name. Senoia has an equally fair share with 'Rock' in the name. Standing Rock. Rock Cut. Rockaway. Rock House. I didn't realize you had to be a geologist to know your way around Senoia. It's a good thing I have a GPS since I was never into the study of minerals.

- Roosters have an internal circadian rhythm that allows them to crow on schedule, which apparently is around 5:25 a.m., or just about the time I'm already eight or nine miles into my morning run. I've been noticing the roosters giving me the stink eye lately.

- Speaking of running, there is nothing I enjoy more (outside of vanilla milkshakes, hanging out with my grandson and seeing the Georgia Bulldogs getting their a**es kicked) than running on country roads. (Yes, this Florida Gator fan knows he's living deep inside enemy territory but that's still better a better option than trying to maneuver around the RV parked in front of the house across the street at O-dark-thirty every morning as I did when I lived in the city.)

- Speaking of running on country roads, I've learned I can run faster than a startled armadillo. From what I've seen so far I'm fairly certain I will be able to say the exact same thing 30 years from now.

- There is no cell phone service at my house. In fact the best I can hope for is one bar of coverage on days when there isn't a cloud in the sky because on those days I can receive text messages on my cell phone. Not *send* them, mind you; just receive them. Apparently the 'dividing line' for cell phone coverage is about a mile from my house because that's where I see cars pulled over on the side of the road so that the driver can finish their phone call before driving any further.

- Being able to see the dark morning sky filled with bright shining stars alone is worth the price of admission.

As for that little issue with cell phone coverage, Cindy and I are in the process of trying to get a landline so we'll be able to reach the outside world. But first we understand someone in Senoia has to forfeit *their* land line to allow us to have theirs.

If I didn't know better I would swear we're now living in Hooterville.

Green Acres we are there.

CHAPTER 40

Psychopathic Symptoms

—————— ∞∞∞ ——————

Face the Truth about Running

I may have an addiction to running. I run every day; every day since November 30, 1978, to be exact. I've begun the last 13,000 or so days of my life by lacing up a pair of running shoes. I've run when the temperature is above 100 degrees and when the temperature is below zero; when I'm feeling on top of the world and when I feel like I'm six feet under; when I've had a good night's sleep and when I've still got beer from last night sloshing around inside my stomach (translation: six feet under). So as I stated earlier: Yes, I may in fact have an addiction to running.

To explore this matter further I decided to take a survey I discovered on Facebook titled 'How much does running rule your life?' I substituted the words 'alcohol' and 'drugs' with 'running' and came to the conclusion the survey was intended to determine whether or not a person had an addiction to running. With that in mind, here's how I did.

There were 50 statements and I was asked to 'check all that apply.' I checked 48 of them. It might be easiest to highlight the two I didn't check:

- Felt a deep sense of shame after skipping a run.

- Successfully snot-rocketed during a run and felt a strange sense of pride.

For that first one, I honestly have no idea. My favorite question when someone finds out about my running streak is 'don't you feel better after you take a day off?' As I said earlier, I wouldn't know.

As for the second one let me assure you: You will never see a snot rocket launched from this nose of mine. I will also never blow my nose at the dinner table and spit in your path if you are running next to me. I may one day live in a barn but I sure as hell wasn't *raised* in one.

As for the 48 items I checked, here's what the survey had to say about me:

> *Wow. You have a problem. Running completely controls your life. I guess in the grand scheme of things, being addicted to running is a good problem to have, but dang. You're probably reading this on a treadmill right now, you psychopath.*

First let me say I have a problem with being told I have a problem, particularly by anyone making the assumption that I was on a treadmill while I took the survey. You wouldn't catch me on a treadmill if every road, sidewalk, path or trail on the planet were covered in six inches of poo and all I had to wear was a brand new $100 pair of running shoes. (By the way, one of the statements was 'spent over $100 on running shoes' which was immediately followed by 'spent a significant amount of money on running accessories.' No one ever said running was cheap. But if you're ever looking to spend your entire inheritance on a *pointless* sport, try golf.)

Other statements that received my seal of approval *(with additional comments added in italics)* were:

- Woken up at an ungodly hour to squeeze in a run. *I set the alarm for 3 a.m. weekdays, 4 a.m. Saturdays and I sleep in on Sundays. (4:30 if you really have to know. I do my long run on Sundays.) I no longer have a grasp on 'ungodly hours.'*

- Ran in the rain…snow…blistering cold. *Actually these were three separate statements in the survey. Of course any runner worth his or her salt has done all three. Other conditions that could have been added and still been checked off include hurricanes, tornados, hailstorms and thunderstorms---complete with lightning, of course. And gale force winds.*

- (Actually five separate statements, but could have been combined into one.) Ran a 5K road race…ran a 10K road race…ran a half marathon…ran a marathon…ran an ultramarathon. *Does a bear run in the woods?*

- Ran twice in one day. *There have been days that I've run three times. Sometimes four. Before breakfast.*

- Ran past midnight. *There isn't a minute in a 24-hour day I haven't been running at some point in my life. Besides, 8 a.m., 12 noon and 4 p.m. are technically all 'after midnight' thus making the statement 'ran past midnight' as the dumbest of the 50 on the survey. Except for the one about 'snot rockets.'*

- Ran while injured even though you knew you should have been resting. *'While hung over, while nursing a stress fracture, while suffering from extreme vertigo and while suffering from beer-sloshing syndrome' could have all been added to the statement and I still would have checked it off.*

- Had to trick yourself to go for a run by promising yourself a reward, like an entire pizza, once you've finished. *Not necessarily a pizza, but most certainly a half-gallon of vanilla ice cream. More than once, I might add. Once in one day, in fact.*

- Had patronizing thoughts towards people who drive cars while running like, 'Look at this guy, driving his car like a frickin' car driver.' *When I'm running early in the morning I believe I own the road and am only willing to defer to a car if it's being driven by someone already finished with their run for the day. Since that* happens about…oh, NEVER I'll leave my 'patronizing thoughts' to your imagination. You may want to dial your imagination setting to 'wildest.'

- Unintentionally donated a toenail to the running gods. *About every six months I make the ultimate sacrifice. I'm convinced my two big toes have an agreement based on 'this town ain't big enough for the both of us' because I never seem to have both toenails at one time. P.S. I just checked. The right one is missing.*

- Been so sore after a long run it was hard to lower yourself onto the toilet. *Or bend over to take off my running shoes. Or pour myself a glass of water. Or towel off after a shower. Or brush my teeth. Or lie down. If dictionaries had pictures, right beneath the word 'sore' would be a picture of, well, probably someone who was very sore (I bet you thought I was going to say 'me,' didn't you? Sorry; my picture is going to be found beneath the word 'psychopath.' Continue.).*

- Crushed a personal record only to be let down when your friends and family didn't throw an entire party in your honor. *I thought reaching 100,000 lifetime miles might do the trick. Or running my 200th marathon. But no, they throw me a party because I had a stupid birthday. Hell, most everyone I know has a birthday. And probably both of their big toenails.*

- Been walking down the street and thought, 'I wish it were socially acceptable to run places instead of walk because this is taking FOREVER.' *I've heard a person burns as many calories walking a mile as they do running a mile. I call 'bullsh*t' because there's no way I burn 100 calories walking a mile. I'm also a little suspicious of the idea of burning 60 calories an hour while I'm asleep because if it were true I wouldn't wake up feeling like a cement mixer was lodged in my stomach after drinking three beers the night before because those calories would theoretically be gone instead of inside said cement mixer. I think biology hates me.*

- Ducked behind a bush or building to relieve yourself during a long run and felt absolutely zero shame. *Since I do most of my running in the dark, ducking behind ANYTHING is a foreign concept to me. Relieving myself, however? I could write a book. Also, it's crossed my mind that I may have in fact been raised in a barn after all.*

CHAPTER 41

What S.I. Jinx?

—⟨∞⟩—

Get my Name in Sports Illustrated

I've been reading *Sports Illustrated* (SI) for over 40 years; in fact it's probably closer to 50 because I remember reading about the Red Sox when Carl Yastrzemski, Tony Conigliaro and Rico Petrocelli were at the heart of the batting order. We were living in Rhode Island at the time and the Red Sox were considered to be our 'home team.' While I never made the trip to Fenway Park (that would come 40 years later), SI's photographs of the Green Monster in left field were larger than life and almost as good as being there in person for one particular wide-eyed 12-year old sporting a buzz cut and a few extra pounds of baby fat.

For well over 2,500 issues I've read every story about baseball, football, basketball, golf, tennis and running that's been featured in the pages of SI. (You may have noticed I didn't mention hockey, automobile racing, hunting, boxing or any of the other sports I don't give a rat's a** about—no disrespect to SI because I'm sure they do a good job of covering them, but they're just not my cup of tea. Once in a while the weekly issue of SI will feature articles about three or four of the sports I just mentioned; I call these issues 'fast forward issues' because it takes me about three minutes to get from cover to cover.) I enjoy all of the regular weekly features the most: Leading Off, Scorecard, Go Figure, Faces in the Crowd and Point After, the article on the back page—especially the ones written a few years back by Rick Reilly before he sold out and left to write for the vastly *inferior ESPN The Magazine.* While it's no secret to the people who know me that Lewis Grizzard is my favorite author, few of them know Rick Reilly runs a close second.

The other regular weekly feature I enjoy reading is Inbox, featuring letters from the readers. I'll be the first to admit: Some of the letters are written so well that if I didn't know better would have thought had been penned by the likes of Frank Deford, Curry Kirkpatrick, Rick Reilly or any of the other prominent and uber successful writers on the SI staff.

So as an aspiring writer since as far back as I can remember, I've always dreamed of the day I too would have a letter published in the pages of SI. I wrote my first letter to SI when I was 15 years old after reading the cover story of 'America's Distance Prodigy,' University of Oregon runner Steve Prefontaine. (At the time I had no idea how important running would be to me one day, but I do know that Pre had a lot to do with my approach to the sport. By the way: The reason I got to visit Fenway Park many years later is because I was in Boston to run a little 26.2-mile race.) I remember how eagerly I waited for the next several issues to be delivered by the mailman, hoping and praying I would see my name printed for the world to see in the pages of the finest sports magazine in the world. Even though my first submission to SI fell on deaf ears (Blind eyes? Uncaring minds?), that didn't stop me from writing again and again through the years.

In 1980 I wrote to SI following the U.S. hockey team's 'Miracle on Ice.' I don't think I've ever been prouder to be an American as I was the day the men's hockey team took the gold medal in the Winter Olympics. At the time I thought my letter contained the most eloquent, from-the-heart words I'd ever written in my life. SI apparently thought otherwise: My letter wasn't printed. Disappointed, I sent my letter to the local newspaper, the *Atlanta Journal-Constitution* only to be rejected yet again. (I have to believe if the letter were submitted to the *AJC* today it would see the light of day. The newspaper has turned into a farce. The newspaper proudly yet erroneously boasts 'Credible, Compelling, Complete' on its front page daily. The morning after this year's college football National Championship game between Florida State and Auburn the front page printed the score after three quarters: Auburn - 21, Florida State - 13. Florida State ultimately won the game and the National Championship on a touchdown pass with 13 seconds left in the game. Credible? Questionable. Complete? Hardly. Come on, say it with me: 'Dewey defeats Truman.')

Through the years I've written to SI whenever I felt inspired, and believe me when I say there were many, many times. Letters about the undefeated 1972 Miami Dolphins; Nolan Ryan's seventh no-hitter at the age of 44 in 1991; Tiger Woods (before he became a punch line) completing his 'Tiger Slam' in 2000; the various magic acts of Michael Jordan; and virtually every rendition of 'March Madness,' the greatest sporting event on earth. There have been others, but after so many rejections a person tends to lose track. I'd guess about three or four dozen would be a pretty good estimate, though.

So when I wrote a letter to SI about an article the published featuring my beloved Florida Gators ('Life After 4-8') and their chances for recovery following their worst football season in many, many years, I wasn't expecting anything in return. A couple weeks later I was reading the September 1st issue and read a letter to the editor and absent mindedly thought 'Gee, this sounds a lot like the letter I wrote to SI' because quite honestly after I submitted it I never gave it another thought (That's what rejection does to a person, people!). Imagine my surprise (and delight) when I read the author of the letter was one Scott Ludwig of Senoia, Georgia (that would be ME for those of you keeping score at home)! If you don't happen to have a copy of the issue handy, fear not: Here is my letter in its (albeit edited) entirety:

> *Florida is the only team scheduled to play both Florida State and Alabama this year—on the road, no less. Here's hoping there really IS life after such a dismal season.*

I know the team is placing a lot of faith in Florida's new offensive coordinator, Kurt Roper to help turn the program around. For the past six years Roper has been the offensive coordinator at Duke and managed to establish a resume that the AJC would be proud of (credible, compelling and complete). While it's too soon to judge if Florida's new hire is paying off, I do know this:

The last time Florida hired an offensive coordinator (he was also their Head Coach) from Duke it turned out pretty well.

His name is Steve Spurrier. You may have heard of him.

Postscript: The 2014 Florida Gators would go on to win six games while losing five. None of the wins were against Alabama and Florida State, and Coach Muschamp was fired nine games into the season.

CHAPTER 42

This 1812 was no War

⸺⸺⸺ ⚬⚬⚬ ⸺⸺⸺

Run with my Grandson in his First Race

I don't know who was more excited this morning: My five-and-a-half year old grandson or his 59-year old G-Pa. But I do know this: We both had the time of our lives.

I've had the pleasure of running with Krischan pretty much since the day he learned to walk. The boy loves to run, and I couldn't be happier. Or prouder, seeing as he 'wants to run just like G-Pa.' In fact Krischan reminds me of my son/his Uncle Josh when he first started running a couple of decades ago. It's been quite a spell between generations, but after today I can honestly say it's been worth the wait.

You see, this morning Krischan ran his first official race and I had the pleasure of being there with him, every hop, step and detour-to-pick-up-miscellaneous-odds- and-ends (baseball, pine cone, dead cicada) along the shady, hilly one-mile route near Spalding Regional Hospital in Griffin, Georgia.

After a busy afternoon and evening yesterday hunting invisible space alien babies in the woods behind the house, finding a jawbone that instantly transformed us into 'scientists' (the 'fossil' was later identified by a Facebook friend as that of a deer) and baking our requisite Friday night batch of peanut butter cookies, I woke up this morning at 3:45 to get in my 10-mile run with my friend Al…while Krischan slept in until 7:30 (our race was at 9:00). Of course no five-and-a-half year old boy 'sleeps in' until 7:30; rather he was woken up early on this Saturday morning by his Yia-Yia (my wife Cindy) to get ready for his racing debut. As you can imagine it wasn't pretty, but after he put on his shorts, shirt and 'running shoes' he couldn't wait to get to the starting line.

'How much further?' I heard more than once as we made the 30-minute drive to Griffin. When we pulled into the parking lot his eyes were as wide as the finishing medal he hoped to have draped around his neck once he crossed his first finish line. I didn't have the heart to tell him there probably wouldn't be a medal for the race (there was an accompanying 5K race—the 'big event;' the one-mile was merely the accompanying 'fun run') but if there wasn't he could choose one of mine when we got back to the house. (He's always admired my medal collection, and one day it is certain to be his.)

We picked up Krischan's race packet and he instantly asked me to pin his race number to the front of his shirt. The number almost covered his entire stomach but that didn't matter to him: He was now an 'official runner.' We walked back to the car to drop off his packet and although I had asked him several times just moments earlier if he needed to use the restroom while we were near the hospital and he said 'no' every time, once we were in the parking lot—with neither a rest room nor porta-pottie anywhere in site—he had to go. *'Now!'* He ran to a tree, dropped his shorts to his ankles and let it fly. It was hard to believe this was the same little boy whom I implored to 'water a tree' last summer in a similar emergency situation and he absolutely refused (I ended up pounding on the door of a local restaurant in Senoia—about two hours before they were open for business and they generously allowed Krischan to use the restroom. His comment as we left: 'This restaurant must not be any good because there aren't any customers.').

All I can figure is it must have been the pressure of running his first race. I asked him as we headed to the starting line what made him so bold; he didn't have an explanation, but as we got close to the gathering of runners he asked me if we could 'stop talking about this now?' After all, it was time to get down to business. Besides, it wasn't a good idea for G-Pa's to embarrass their grandsons when they were about to compete in an athletic competition for the first time.

As we waited at the back of a pack of 100 or so runners (the 5K and the one-mile started simultaneously, but the two races took different routes) I told Krischan not to start out too fast because, after all, a mile is a really long way. Over the years Krischan has covered as many as three miles with me, but as you might imagine not all of it was running: There was always a good amount of walking, talking to neighbors and petting every dog that crossed our path. But today would be different: Today was all about *running*.

As the Race Director was going over the instructions for the races, Krischan asked if we could hold hands while we ran. 'You know, so you can keep up with me, G-Pa.' I told him he would need to have his hands free so his arms could pump as he ran, but I would do my absolute best to keep up with him.

Krischan started off exactly as I asked: Conservative pace, arms-a-pumping and cheeks turning bright red as he crested the first of several hills on one of the more challenging 'fun run' courses I've ever seen. Let me be the first to say the experience was wonderful: He smiled the entire time, slowed down only for a couple of steps because his 'stomach hurt' and even managed to squeeze in a little exploration and housekeeping along the way. Krischan waved to everyone along the course and got excited every time someone shouted him encouragement ('Do they know me, G-Pa? They must because they're cheering for me!').

We played leapfrog with several other runners for most of the race. As you probably already guessed I took my fair share of photos along the way so I could have a record of this special morning. As we neared the finish line, by my calculation we were in the middle of a pack of about 25 runners, walkers, moms, dads and one lone G-Pa. I told Krischan he should cross the finish line in front of me because I wasn't wearing a number, but he would have none of it: We would be crossing the finish line together. I think what he said was 'Catch up to me, G-Pa; I'll slow down so you can' which was his subtle way of reminding me I'm not as young as him (he thinks I'm 25, by the way).

We ran the final 10 or so glorious steps together and crossed Krischan's first finish line in an official time of eighteen minutes and twelve seconds. 18:12, a time that is now part of my vernacular along with 76:36 (a 10-mile race Josh ran when he was nine years old), 3:18:15 (Cindy's first half-marathon) and 36:14 (my 10K best). I imagine when my memory starts failing me—I'm guessing around the time I'm running my great-grandchild's first race with him or her—the time I'll still remember will be 18:12.

While Krischan may not remember his finishing time, I have high hopes that he'll always remember the day he ran just like his G-Pa.

Postscript: Six weeks later I paced Krischan in his second one-mile race. He ran—all 5,280 feet—and lowered his time by almost eight minutes, finishing in 12 minutes and 21 seconds. The next time out he lowered his time to 11 minutes and 11 seconds. It won't be long before he'll be running faster than his G-Pa.

CHAPTER 43

In my Skin

———— ❧ ————

Streak...the Old-Fashioned Way

It's no secret I run every single day, which qualifies me as a 'streaker.' What remains a secret to most everyone except for a very small circle of friends is that I am also a streaker. Yes, that means exactly what you think it means: I have run nekkid.

Although almost 40 years have passed since those ten minutes of alcohol-induced spontaneity that took me on a circuitous route from my dormitory room through the women's dormitory next door and around the Arts and Sciences Building (where ironically four years later I would have an office on the second floor as a Graduate Teaching Assistant) and then through the Rathskellar (the on-campus bar) and finally up three flights of stairs back to where I started. I must mention I had an accomplice: My dorm mate and best friend from high school was with me--every sip and every step of the way. I was 18 years old and as you probably already surmised 'common sense' was the farthest thing from my mind.

Four decades later I'm not the same person I was in college. I've gained a lot of wisdom and common sense over the years (although my wife might suggest otherwise) and now run every day wearing clothes.

Except today, that is.

Today, as I did as a freshman at the University of Florida on a rather chilly Friday night in the fall so long ago, I ran along the streets of _____ (city/state/country intentionally omitted to prevent possible criminal action in the future) wearing nothing but a pair of New Balance running shoes and a smile (and a flashlight to alert oncoming cars that I was running along the side of the road). Originally I wanted to run nekkid legally; I was planning on running in a race at a nudist colony in north Georgia last spring. In the past I had been invited by the Race Director--more than once, as a matter of fact--to run in the Fig Leaf 5K but decided against it each time, seeing as I had all of this wisdom and common sense swelling up inside of me and all. But this year I decided it was time to give it a try, but by the time I inquired about it the race had already been held. I missed it by a couple of days, which led me to where I was this morning: Running along the streets of _____ (irritating, isn't it?) on a dark _____ (chilly, warm, tepid, foggy, rainy, windy--conditions intentionally omitted; you know why) morning...butt nekkid.

OK, so I didn't run the entire 10 miles this morning that way. I ran a few miles, removed everything I was wearing but my shoes, and ran a good 10-minutes or so down the road with only three concerns in mind: Whether or not I would be recognized, arrested or experience any pain caused by (for lack of a better term) 'package slappage.'

Ten minutes into the 'natural' portion of my run I was ready to turn around and head back: Back to my pile of stashed clothing, back to where I started running au naturale and back to reality. But then the thought occurred to me: To be truly 'at one with nature' my feet should be touching Mother Earth. Besides, I was thinking back to earlier this year when I spent the day with my grandson and he wanted me to take him running. I noticed he was wearing flip-flops and told him he couldn't run in them. He insisted on running, so I asked him what he would be running in since all he had was flip-flops. I can still hear his reply: 'In my feet.'

So with one shoe in either hand I ran the last 10 minutes of my au naturale run, stopping only to pull the occasional impediment (pebble/piece of glass/Kryptonite--hard to tell in the dark) out of my foot. It made me think back to when I lived in Hawaii and wearing shoes was the exception rather than the rule. Over the course of the three years I lived on Oahu the bottoms of my feet developed a leathery almost reptilian quality to them; a time when I didn't give a second thought to walking barefoot on broken glass. But my feet couldn't compare to the feet of the legendary Randall Tanaka, a classmate of mine at Moanalua Intermediate School. Randall's feet were so tough he could walk barefoot through fire, a fact I know to be true because I saw him do it. I was the Senior Patrol Leader of our Boy Scout Troop and after a Tuesday night meeting we built a campfire to roast marshmallows and a few other objects I don't care to talk about here. Randall boasted to some of the Scouts he could stand barefoot on the open fire for as long as it took to toast a marshmallow, and after just the right amount of laughter--and wagering--he hopped into the fire and stepped from one burning log to the next while everyone else literally sat around the campfire, their mouths wide open and blank stares on their faces as Randall told them to 'pay up, suckers!' On the way home from the meeting Randall and I stopped at a department store and he used his winnings to buy a box of 24 giant Sweet Tarts, one of the four major food groups of Troop # 201.

Interesting aside: In my entire career in both Cub and Boy Scouts I went camping only once. It was my first year in Cub Scouts in Quonset Point, Rhode Island. It was only one night alone in the woods, but it left considerable emotional scars. I built a lean-to in which to sleep and store my belongings. If you're not familiar with a lean-to I suggest you watch the first episode of any given season of 'Survivor' and see what the tribes build out of branches and palm fronds for shelter. What you'll see makes the castaways of 'Gilligan's Island' look like the Frank Lloyd Wright's of island architecture. The only difference between the huts built by the contestants on Survivor and my lean-to is this: Their huts have roofs that leak while my lean-to was open on one side and allowed four inches of snow to accumulate during the night.

It makes me wonder how I ever made Senior Patrol Leader, a fact I find almost as ironic as putting the finishing touches on a graduate degree within the walls of a building I had run around bare-a** naked a few years earlier.

So once I got back to my pile of clothes on the side of the road and dressed in total darkness (try to distinguish between your right shoe and your left shoe in the dark sometime; not as easy as you might think) I headed back to _____ (come on; you didn't think I was going to slip up NOW, did you?) and hopped in the shower, wondering whether or not I would ever mention what I'd done over the past 90 minutes.

And now you're well aware what I decided to do: Write it down for the world to see!

Maybe my wife has the right idea after all. I may be a little light on the wisdom and common sense, but I'm also pretty light on my feet.

Especially when I'm not wearing any clothes.

CHAPTER 44

Epicenter of the Universe

—∞∞∞—

Visit Pittsburgh

Considering my parents grew up in the little town of Birdsboro and were life-long fans of the Phillies and the Eagles of Philadelphia—about 40 miles to the southeast by way of Pottstown—I never ventured to the west side of the great state of Pennsylvania. That's because on the west side of the state is where you would find Pittsburgh.

Located over 400 miles to the west, the only thing I knew about Pittsburgh was that it was known as the Evil Empire long before the phrase entered into the mind of a certain individual by the name of George Lucas. Philadelphia is known as the 'City of Brotherly Love.' Pittsburgh, on the other hand is known by several nicknames. 'The Steel City.' 'The City of Bridges.' The one I remember from my youth? 'Sh*ttsburgh,' because I heard my dad say it once after the Pirates beat the Phillies in extra innings. I can still remember riding in the car for a really long time with my Aunt Freda and innocently asking her if we were 'going all the way to Sh*ttsburgh.' She pulled over to the shoulder of the turnpike and prayed for my soul. I was six years old at the time.

I'm discussing Pittsburgh for a reason: I finally had the opportunity to visit and see the city for myself, thanks to our annual work summit being held along the banks of the Allegheny River in—according to my boss—the

'Epicenter of the Universe,' which for me is a dead giveaway the man has never traveled outside of our immediate solar system. We're staying in the Renaissance Pittsburgh Hotel and from our meeting room you can look across the river and see the playing field at PNC Park, home of those damn Phillies-beating Pirates. Someone told me PNC Park has been designated 'the most romantic ballpark in the country.' That took me by surprise: Not because it's in Pittsburgh but rather because I have a hard time understanding how watching 18 grown men stand around for three hours spitting tobacco chewing and adjusting their respective crotches could even *remotely* be considered 'romantic.'

One night we rode on the 'Duquesne Incline,' a cable car built in 1877 to the top of Mount Washington so we could enjoy dinner with a view of the city that lights up in black and gold whenever one of the local teams (Pirates, Steelers, University of Pittsburgh Panthers) win a game. Although I have an inherent fear of heights, riding in cable cars has never bothered me. The Duquesne Incline didn't bother me either, especially since we were never more than four or five feet above the side of the mountain. What unnerved me about the Duquesne Incline was—as I said earlier built in 1877 and as far as I could tell was still maintained by its original hardware and machinery. If you have any doubt take a ride on it sometime and just listen.

Another night we had dinner at the Penn Brewery, located directly across the street from the Heinz factory. The Penn Brewery offered a varied selection of locally-brewed beers (all deemed very good by our self-appointed band of beer critics) and the dinner menu offered a variety of German fare, most of them containing red meat in some way, shape or form. Since I'm into my fifth year of foregoing red meat I ordered a veggie burger and fries. (Note: On business trips to Germany eating in restaurants presents a challenge. I usually stick to a fairly healthy diet of sauerkraut, spaetzle (noodles and cheese) and salads (German salads are *wonderful*)... and trips to as many German bakeries as I can possibly find.) OK, back to the veggie burger...

The other 19 people in my party (we're all sitting at one looong table) order wiener schnitzel with various combinations of sides -- -red cabbage, sauerkraut, German potato salad, spaetzle—all of which the waitress remembers exactly as to who got what ('Let's see, you had the wiener schnitzel with red cabbage and sauerkraut but no spaetzle...you had the Weiner schnitzel with red cabbage and spaetzle but no sauerkraut...you had the wiener schnitzel with spaetzle and a German salad on the side,' etc.) I was amazed the waitress could remember 19 different variations of the same menu item, so it caught me by surprise when she yelled loud enough for workers at the Heinz factory to hear 'Who got the veggie burger with fries?' Believe me, there's nothing like drawing attention to the one guy in a German restaurant who doesn't eat red meat. He's the guy who is looked at like he might be carrying the Black Plague.

One afternoon we took a tour of the city courtesy of Just Ducky Tours. We boarded a military DUKW (an amphibious vehicle from the Second World War) and drove all around Pittsburgh as well as *through* Pittsburgh on the Ohio River ('amphibious' means to be able to use either land or water, something you should have learned in the fifth grade). The tour was informative and honestly a lot of fun if you don't count the many times he asked us to 'quack three times' at random strangers along the tour route. Do you know how embarrassing it is for a group of 20 adults to make a young girl cry by screaming at her like a duck? I do; three times over, in fact.

After spending three days in the Steel City I think my dad may have been wrong. The city has charm. The city has personality. Most of all the city has pretty much anything you could ask for in a major metropolis, and most of it you can reach by foot.

Looking back on those three days in western Pennsylvania I'm not sure I would consider Pittsburgh to be a big little city or a little big city, but I do know one thing:

Dad had it all wrong.

BONUS TRACK
JUST PLAIN STUPID

I've seen a lot of things in my life that were just plain stupid. Granted, I was responsible for most of them; just not *all* of them. Here are a few that instantly come to mind every time I hear the joke about a redneck's last words being 'bet you've never seen anyone do *this* before!'

1. I was at a cookout and the man responsible for grilling the hot dogs had no feeling in either hand. Apparently he fell backwards off a ladder at some point in his life and broke his fall by stretching out his arms, thus landing on his palms and destroying the nerves in both hands in the process. What that translated to was his 'talent' for cooking the hot dogs on a hot, flaming grill by rolling them with his bare hands since he wasn't able to feel the heat. The fire, however had another effect on him:

Me: *You realize both of your hands are in the fire, right?*
Him: (Boldly, because his chest was puffed out) *Yes, but I don't feel a thing.*
Me: *Maybe so, but your flesh appears to be melting.*

2. There was a man who voluntarily ran across Death Valley, over two mountain ranges and all the way to the portals of Mount Whitney, a distance of 135 miles. It was in mid-July and the temperatures reached the low 130's. It took him over 36 hours. But he finished, dammit. He finished. (OK, so this one was *me*.)

3. The route I drive to work through a small town in Georgia crosses a train track. Once in a while the train comes and when it does the railroad is blocked off by those big wooden arms with the flashing lights. When that happens I--as well as every single other driver I've seen in the last 11 years--turn right, drive about half a mile, turn left onto a road that runs beneath the train tracks and merge back onto my normal route. Simple. However one day when the wooden arms with the flashing lights were staring me in the face, I happened to be the third vehicle 'in line.' The two vehicles in front of me apparently were content to wait out the train; I wasn't. I pulled around the two cars and turned right, just like anyone else save these two yahoos in front of me on this particular day would have done. Big mistake: The first vehicle in line was a police car. Instinctively I pulled over to the curb, about a nanosecond before the flashing blue lights signaled me to. The policeman got out of his car, walked up to my window and said 'give me your license so I can write you a ticket.' He walked back to his car and returned 30 seconds later and asked me why I would pull around a policeman at a stop sign and turn in front of him. I said I--as well as every single other driver I'd seen in the last 11 years--did it all the time when a train came through. The policeman then retaliated with perhaps the worst (translation: dumbest) analogy in the history of the English language by asking: *'If a policeman was watching and everyone was jumping off of the top of a building, would YOU?'* Shortly thereafter he returned my license to me and told me to *'go on...just go on.'* I consider myself fortunate this occurred at 6:58 a.m. on a Thursday morning, or two minutes before the policeman's shift was over. His police station was directly on the other side of the railroad tracks, coincidentally.

4. Once upon a time I had a root canal. Without any anesthetic. The end.

5. When Cindy and I were dating, we spent one summer at my parent's house in Virginia. One night we went out to see a movie and on the way home decided to stop for a few minutes to park *(Is*

that what they still call it? Parking?) in my parent's subdivision in an area where new houses were being built. It was raining--heavily-- and the dirt we parked in soon turned into mud. Once we realized our car was stuck in that mud, I walked to a neighbor's house and asked for their help. I didn't bother asking for their silence because I thought that was understood. The neighbors were able to help us get our car out of the mud that night, and 12 or 13 years later my parents finally let me in on their little secret: They knew about it the very night it happened. Moral of the story? Don't park in the mud.

6. There was a man who voluntarily ran 100 miles through the Sierra Nevada mountain range on a route that went up-and-down-and-up-and-down-and-up-and-down. And up. This man had no business running through the mountains, since most of his training miles were run on asphalt. The course was exceptionally wet and the man's running shoes stayed saturated for 30 hours. At the end of the run the man had a deep gash right down the middle of the ball of his left foot. The best description of the foot is this: If the bottom of the foot was the state of Arizona; then the deep gash would be the Grand Canyon. Yes, it was *that deep!* (Me again.)

7. Did you notice I didn't mention the name of the small town in #3? That's because the men and women of the Fairburn Police Department don't have a sense of humor.

8. In sixth grade I was sitting in the back of the classroom next to my best friend. Abruptly he lifted his right leg and passed gas so *passionately* (I don't know what else to call it) that it rumbled--LOUDLY--in his wooden chair and echoed throughout the classroom. I put my face down on my desk because I just knew I was going to laugh until I cried. Thirty seconds later I lifted my head and saw every single face in the classroom looking directly at me. I glanced over to my best friend and found him solemnly pointing at me--as if he was disgusted I would do such a thing.

9. It is entirely possible to trip over a quarter-inch rise in the asphalt while running. It is also entirely possible to run two miles in 12 minutes with blood gushing out of a one-inch gash directly beneath your chin. I hate that I know these things to be true.

10. It is entirely possible to forget the names of people you've known for two generations. I hate that I know this to be true as well.

Looking back over this list, perhaps I'm confusing 'stupid' with 'getting older.' Maybe there's hope for me yet.

The policeman in Fairburn, however, doesn't stand a chance.

CHAPTER 45

Take One for the Team

∽∘∘∘∽

Fly Solo at Music Trivia

I've been playing music trivia one night a week since the spring of 2005. Originally our team name was 'the Rockin' B's,' named after an antique shop owned by one of our team members. When she left the team a new name was selected: The Fried Mushrooms. (I wasn't playing on that fateful night, because if I was I would have named our team 'In First Place' because I thought it would create a lot of confusion when the DJ announced each team's point totals after each round of songs: *'In third place is In First Place with 36 points.'* Shades of 'who's on first,' no?). We've had the name ever since, although I abbreviate it to the much cooler and less syllabic 'FM.'

Over the years our core group of seven or eight players has remained the same, although on any given night we've had as many as 23 players on our team and as few as three. On the night we had 23 players we took first place, but when you consider we won a $30 gift certificate to the restaurant hosting the music trivia and that $30 divided 23 ways equates to $1.30 each, one might question if we really 'won' since our winnings couldn't even cover our tips for the waitress. (Basic Rule of Music Trivia: Always keep your waitresses happy because they are a good resource if any songs of the past decade are played that no one on the team listens to because in all honesty today's music is pretty sorry.)

However, this week was the first time the Fried Mushrooms team consisted of a party of one. The 'one' in question was me. It was no party.

After a couple of weeks of 'easy weeks' (as the music trivia host calls them) it was time for a 'hard week.' I've played somewhere in the neighborhood of 400+ games of music trivia and have a pretty good sense of what is easy and what is hard. But I'll be the first to admit that tonight was by far the toughest game yet.

The format is simple: Four rounds of four songs each. Identify the song title, artist and third question (varies) and each part is worth three points; get all three correct and you get a bonus point for a possible total of 10 points per song. At the end of the night there is a Jeopardy-style wager round where you can bet all of your points, some of your points but no less than one point. Top three teams win gift cards ($30 for first, $20 for second and $10 for third).

Here's the play-by-play with all the gory details:

Round One: Actors pretending to be Singers (identify the song title, artist and a random third question)

Song #1: *Party all the Time*, Eddie Murphy and 1985. Third question was year of release +/- one year. No problem with this one—especially after hearing the title repeated over and over and over (and over). All three correct: 10 points.

Song #2: *Hang Tough*, New Kids on the Block and Joey McIntyre. First two were correct; third question was which band member appeared on Broadway. I wrote down Justin Timberlake even though I knew he wasn't in NKOTB but rather in Sync or Backstreet Boys or Boyz2Men—am I even spelling these correctly? Don't know and don't care enough to check. Anyway I knew either NKOTB or Timberlake would be a correct answer and I was right: 6 points.

Song #3: *The Kill*, 30 Seconds to Mars and Jared Leto. Third question was which band member stars in movies. I got everything right but the song title—I thought it might be *Killing Me*---which was disappointing because I love the song but in all honesty I quit learning song titles in the mid-'90's because that's pretty much when music died for me: 6 points.

Song #4: *Cups*, Anna Kendrick, *Pitch Perfect*. Third question was name the movie the song was featured in. I never heard the song before in my life--I guessed *When I'm Gone* because it was repeated as many times as Eddie Murphy's *Party All theTime*--and I never saw the movie. I was the only team that didn't get this one right: 0 points.

After round I was in 4ᵗʰ place (out of five teams) with 22 points, 14 behind the first place team. As ugly as it was, it wasn't the end of the world. That would come a little bit later.

Round Two: Songs without Lyrics (song title, artist and a random third question)

Song #1: *Green Onions*, Booker T and the MG's, *Oceans 11*. Third question was name the movie the song was featured in. I got credit for all three being correct, but in all honesty I wasn't sure about *Oceans 11*. I looked it up later and it was NOT in the movie. I think I was given credit for a right answer because of how fast I turned my answer in…and because the song *should* have been in *Oceans 11*. It was actually in *The Sandlot*: 10 points.

Song #2: *Jessica*, Allman Brothers Band and 1971. Third question was year of release +/- one year. I guessed *In Memory of Elizabeth Reed* as the song title but it was the *other* Allman Brothers instrumental—in fact I wrote down *Jessica* before I changed my answer: 3 points.)

Song #3: *Sirius*, Alan Parsons Project, Chicago Bulls. Third question was which team used the song for their entrance. I guessed the theme from *2001: A Space Odyssey*. It probably would have helped me rule it out if I'd ever seen the movie. I also guessed the artist as Vangelis; I totally made that up: 3 points.

Song #4: *Eruption*, Van Halen and 1978. Third question was year of release +/- one year. At least I recognized Eddie Van Halen's guitar, but I guessed it was Sammy Hagar Van Halen and said 1985. I was wrong; it was David Lee Roth Van Halen: 3 points.)

After round 2 I was tied for third, 28 points out of first place. Halftime is worth 20 points if you 'check in' on Facebook (10 points) and correctly answer the 'this day in music history question' (10 points). I got all 20 points but remain 28 points out.

As for the halftime question: The three members of ZZ Top bought plane tickets in 1987 for the first flight to where? The correct answer: The moon.

Fun fact #1: I saw ZZ Top for the first time in the early '70's when I was in high school in Florida. They opened for Grand Funk Railroad. None of the band members were sporting a beard at the time.

Fun fact #2. ZZ Top is famous for the long beards of Billy Gibbons and Dusty Hill, the lead and bass guitarists, respectively. Know which band member *doesn't* sport a beard? The drummer. His name? Frank Beard.

Round 3: Where in the World? (song title, artist and country artist is from)

Song #1: *Raining on Sunday*, Keith Urban and Australia. What can I say? I hate country music and just wanted to get on to the next question. I did manage to hear the song title through the blood that was pouring out of my ears, however. I also knew there was a country singer who wasn't from the USA but for the life of me I couldn't remember the name Keith Urban so I wrote down USA. Next time I won't forget. That's a lie; I'll have forgotten by tomorrow: 3 points.

Song #2: *Celebration*, Led Zeppelin and England. It's hard to believe I missed the name of a Led Zep song (I wrote *Brontysaur Stomp*). Did you notice I spelled 'brontysaur' wrong? If you didn't, you may now step off your high horse because you're no more of a Led Zeppelin expert than I am: 6 points.

Song #3: *Magic Carpet Ride*, Steppenwolf and Canada. Canada! Who knew? Not me, obviously; I said USA. If you knew Steppenwolf was from Canada, you may now return to your high horse because I won't be needing it: 6 points.

Song #4: *Ruby Tuesday*, Rolling Stones and England. Would you believe some of the teams thought the song was by the Beatles? I sh*t thee not: 10 points.

After round 3 I fell back into fourth place, a whopping 39 points behind the leading team. It's not looking good for the home team.

Round 4: Bad Girls (song title, artist featuring a female singer and year of release +/- one year)

Song #1: *Spider Web*, No Doubt and 1995 I took my son Josh to see No Doubt for his 10th birthday...in 1995. Good memory for years; not so much for song titles: 6 points.)

Song #2: *The Seether*, Veruca Salt and 1994. Not only did I guess the artist was Garbage (the group, not the stuff in your trash can), but also that the song was older but I must have been thinking about me instead of the song (1987). This song was played a couple months ago and I swore I would remember Veruca Salt. I lied. To myself, but I still lied: 3 points.)

Song #3: *Paranoia*, Garbage and 1998. I figured if I kept writing down 'Garbage' it was bound to be right sooner or later. The name of the song? *The Seether* would have been a better guess than *Bend Me*. As for the year being 11 years off (I guessed 1987), I could have sworn Garbage was hot during the MTV decade of the '80's. That's what I get for thinking: 3 points.)

Song #4: *Salvation*, Cranberries and 1996. I guessed the year as 1993. I won't be losing any sleep over this one because I wasn't sure which album the song was on. Time for the final round: 6 points.

After round 4 I was still in fourth place, an embarrassing 61 points behind the leaders. The point totals of the five teams at this point were: 165, 125, 115, 104 (that would be me) and 95. The bonus round was announced as 'movie theme songs without any lyrics.' I wager 61 points, which would beat the leading team by one point if they only bet one point and I answered the bonus round correctly and everyone else didn't. Sometimes you have to dream…

Bonus Round: Fifteen movie theme songs—20 seconds of each were played. To receive your wagered points you have to get at least 9 of the movies correct.

Here's what my answer sheet looked like:

1.
2.
3.
4.
5.
6.
7.
8.
9.
10.
11.
12.
13.
14. *Titanic*
15.

The good news: Not ONE SINGLE TEAM answered the question correctly (that is to say, identify at least nine of the 15 theme songs).

The bad news: Had I only bet ONE POINT I would have finished in FIRST PLACE!

The ugly news: I don't know sh*t about movie theme songs without lyrics. Whatever happened to the good old days? *Tubular Bells* by Mike Oldfield in *The Exorcist*. *The Entertainer* by Marvin Hamlisch in *The Sting*. You know, the songs people *knew* and the movies people *saw!*

Here are the theme songs I (and apparently everyone else) missed. If you've seen any of these movies, take a minute and hum the theme song to yourself. Having trouble? Exactly.

- *Forrest Gump* (admittedly I should have known this one, but that would have only given me two correct answers because I didn't know any of the rest)

- *Harry Potter: The Prisoner of Such-and-Such* (not sure if I saw this one; I saw one Harry Potter film but don't ask me which)

- *Back to the Future* (haven't seen it in a generation or more)

- *Sherlock Holmes* (haven't seen it in this lifetime)

- *The Avengers* (it had a theme song?)

- *Last of the Mohicans* (isn't this a documentary?)

- *How to Train your Dragon* (if only my grandson had been playing with me tonight)

- *Tron: Legacy* (seriously?)

- *Stardust* (the DJ said—and I quote—'I've never even heard of this movie.' Then WHY PLAY IT?)

- *National Treasure* (never saw it; honest)

- *October Sky* (never heard of it)

- *Inception* (will get around to watching it one of these days; unfortunately that day wasn't today)

- *Titanic* (I totally nailed this one)

- *Lord of the Rings: Fellowship of This-and-That* (hard for me to tell any of these movies apart—much yet the theme songs)

So, as I asked before: How many of these can you hum? Yeah, me neither.

CHAPTER 46

Nevermore

————— ⚮ —————

Attend an American Football Conference Team's Home Game

I've been to two professional football games in my entire life. Both of them were in Atlanta, and both of them had the National Football Conference's Atlanta Falcons on one side of the ball, so that sort of contradicts the 'professional' part of that first sentence.

That being said I witnessed my first professional football game hosted by a team in the *American* Football Conference when I saw the Baltimore Ravens host the Carolina Panthers (once again challenging the meaning of the word 'professional') in M & T Bank Stadium in the former stomping grounds of Edgar Allen Poe. I was visiting my sister who just so happens to have two season tickets to all of the Ravens' games and since—for the first time in all of my visits to Baltimore during football season—I was in town and the Ravens had a home game, she invited me to go to the game with her. My sister, well aware that I will never spend one red cent on professional sports, agreed to pay for any expenses we might incur (had it not been for her hunger pangs in the third quarter there wouldn't have been any; I'm a cheap date).

Figuring I had nothing to lose—outside of the eight hours required to watch a three-hour football game as I would soon find out—I told her to count me in.

I know what you're thinking. *'Eight hours for a three-hour game? How could that be?'*

Real quick:

9:00 a.m.   We drove to the stadium. Miraculously we avoided any traffic jams, accidents or mobs consisting of overly-optimistic Panther fans.

9:30 a.m.   We met friends in the parking lot and socialized; drank a beer. Correction: Beers.

10:30 a.m.   We toured vendor booths and exhibits; drank more beer. Correction: Much more.

11:30 a.m.   We walked the perimeter of the stadium looking for a friend whom we later discovered watched the game in a bar located 20 miles away; drank beer to combat possible dehydration on a sunny and unseasonably warm day. Correction: It's totally within reason to assume we were searching for a porta-john as well as looking for her friend, seeing as beers are nothing more than rental commodities.

12:45 p.m.   We entered the stadium and found our seats; everyone was dressed in purple and/or black (the official Raven team colors). Correction: Everyone but me.

Regarding the color purple: Purple and white were the colors of my high school, Duncan U. Fletcher Senior High in Neptune Beach, Florida. Go Fighting Senators!

I hate the color purple. I haven't worn it since high school. I loathe the Minnesota Vikings and the LSU Tigers in some part because one of their team colors is purple. I've never seen 'The Color Purple.' Two reasons: Oprah and Winfrey. I'm not a fan. In fact I'm not a fan of her spinoff talk shows hosted by two of her disciples, Dr. Oz and Dr. Phil. In fact one of the marching orders for my dental hygienist is to make sure my 4:00 appointment (during which she has the Ellen DeGeneres Show turned on—which is totally fine because she—Ellen, not my dental hygienist is the funniest lady on the planet) is over before 5:00 because that is when the Dr. Phil show begins. If I'm still in the dentist's office when Dr. Phil's big, shiny head takes the stage I'm free to walk.

1:00 p.m.   Kickoff. It didn't take long to determine I was correct in implying Carolina was not a professional team.

1:01 p.m. until 3:59 p.m.   I heard the refrain from the White Stripes' *Seven Nation Army* so many times I fear I may vomit the next time I hear the song in its entirety.

4:00 p.m.   Ravens 38, Panthers 10. It wasn't nearly as close as it sounds. Carolina was pathetic.

4:05 p.m.   We left the stadium. Miraculously we avoided any traffic jams, accidents or mobs consisting of vengeful Panther fans.

5:00 p.m.   We're back at my sister's house; I realized the game consumed eight hours of my life I'll never get back.

However I have to admit the day had a few bright spots:

- I met some of the notable Baltimore fans, including Raven Man and June Cleavage (don't ask), every last one of them decked out from head to toe in purple and black feathers, various Spandex accessories and some semblance of a beak. *(Yes, I had my photo taken with most of them. Why? Pure and simple: Beer. Correction: Lots of beer.)*

- I took my very first 'selfie' standing beneath the new statue of Ray Lewis outside of the stadium. The photograph presents the illusion that Lewis is about to stomp on my head. *(Note: About four hours and seven or eight beers later my head felt like it had been stomped—repeatedly—by the entire Raven defensive unit.)*

- I adopted a real raven (black feathers, a beak, no Spandex) at a booth hosted by the Baltimore Zoo. In my mind his name is 'Edgar,' my personal tribute to the famous author of the poem 'The Raven.'

- Steve Smith of the Ravens was the difference maker in the game, catching two touchdown passes including a deflected pass he caught in stride for the game's first score. It was payback time as the Panthers released Smith a year ago and—judging by the comments Smith made in the week following the game—there are lots of bad blood between he and the Panther front office. I love a good vengeance story *('I was stabbed in the back,'* Smith said after the game in reference to how he had been treated by the Panthers).

- A Raven fan several rows directly in front of me—obviously having consumed about three times as much alcohol as I—miraculously avoided falling headfirst over the railing and into the end zone, eliciting many 'oooh's' and 'ahhh's' from the hometown crowd throughout the game.

- I only saw one Ray Rice jersey the entire day. For all I know it might have been him.

So to be fair, the day wasn't a total loss.

That is, unless you were a Carolina Panther.

As to whether or not I'll ever attend another professional football game, feel free to ask the raven of Edgar Allen Poe and he'll gladly tell you:

Nevermore.

CHAPTER 47

Kid in the Hall

Visit the College Football Hall of Fame

Given the choice between a chocolate candy bar and a tomato, he'd opt for the healthier choice and grab the vegetable...and ask for seconds.

Given the choice between spending the day at the circus or a two-hour trip to the museum, dinosaur bones and prehistoric cave art trump red-nosed clowns and high-flying acrobats every time.

Given the choice between sitting on the couch to watch cartoons or going for a run, he'd rather lace up his tiny running shoes even though it would be much simpler to slip on a pair of tiny alligator bedroom slippers.

If I've learned one thing about my grandson Krischan, it's that he is prone to say or do the exact opposite of what most people would expect. You can include me in that category, even though by now I should know better. My wife Cindy and I took Krischan to Atlanta's brand new College Football Hall of Fame—through a special offer from the Atlanta Gator Club—and expected his tolerance level for 'all things football' to be somewhere in the neighborhood of four or five minutes. As our tour was scheduled to last two hours, our apprehension about taking Krischan with us is understandable.

A little background: Krischan has been exposed to 'all things Gator' since the day he was born. I won't go into detail but let's just say everything from his first onesie to his first stuffed gator to his first sippie cup has been orange and blue. He's been doing the Gator 'chomp' since he was two. He can instantly recognize the Gator football team when they're playing on TV. And yes, he can yell 'Go Gators!' at the top of his lungs with the best of us. The boy was born to bleed orange and blue.

But two solid hours of NBF (nothing but football)? Was it too much for a boy not yet six years old? Let's find out, shall we?

4:00 – 4:05 p.m. We met our tour guide Terry LeCount, former NFL player and more importantly former Florida Gator. Terry was the quarterback at Florida when Cindy and I were students there. In fact Terry played quarterback in high school at Raines, one of the archrival schools in Jacksonville, Florida of Duncan U. Fletcher, the alma mater of Cindy and I. How did my high school fare in football against Terry's alma mater? Let's just say the Raines mascot was a Viking and the Fletcher mascot was a Senator: Now imagine the two of them squaring off. Yeah, it was ugly. Truth be known Fletcher Senior High was located at the beach and in a perfect world our school mascot would be Jeff Spicoli, the surfer dude from *Fast Times at Ridgemont High ('All I need are some tasty waves, a cool buzz and I'm fine.')*.

4:05 – 4:20 p.m. We listened to our special guest Danny Wuerffel, former NFL player, former Florida Gator and former Heisman Trophy Winner (1996). Danny led the Gators to four consecutive SEC Championships (1993 – 1996) and a National Championship in his senior year. Danny told some old war stories from his days playing for the 'Evil Genius,' former Florida Head Coach Steve Spurrier. Although I've heard the stories before I still find myself laughing— probably because Danny's impersonation of Spurrier is so spot-on accurate with his rat-a-tat delivery and scrunched up nose—that I can practically envision Steve himself up on the stage. My favorite story from Danny's repertoire (I'm paraphrasing here):

I was a freshman at Florida and pretty nervous playing in front of such a large crowd for the first time. I called a basic pass play that allowed the receiver a multitude (I counted seven as Danny spoke) *of variations in the route he would be running. As I called the signals at the line I audibled to announce which of the routes the receiver should run. I threw the football exactly where the receiver should have been, but the receiver turned 'in' when he should have turned 'out' and the pass was intercepted. I was really afraid to go to the sideline because I feared what Coach would have to say; I was just hoping he realized the interception was the receiver's mistake and not mine. I ran up to him and said 'sorry, coach' and he replied back: 'It's not your fault, Danny. It's mine...for putting you out there in the first place.'*

After Danny spoke we had the opportunity to meet him, but seeing how long the line was we opted for seeing a 10-minute video of what it's like on the sideline, in the huddle and on the field of an NCAA football game. Krischan seemed to like it because there was a fair share of Gator players throughout the film. Afterwards we returned to stand in a still fairly long line to meet Danny. Once we got to the head of the line Cindy got Danny's autograph on two posters we picked up on the way in (a cartoon alligator chasing after a cartoon bulldog—perfect since the annual Florida-Georgia game was only seven days away).

Krischan did Cindy one better. Danny picked him up, sat Krischan down next to him on the side of the stage, posed for a couple of photographs and spoke to him directly for a good 90 seconds. Looking at the photographs later, you would have thought Krischan was sitting on a nail rather than sitting next to a former Heisman Trophy Winner. Danny was fighting a winless battle trying to coax a 'Go Gators!' out of him.

4:20 – 5:20 p.m. This was where Krischan's patience was put to the test. We were touring the actual Hall of Fame. (When Krischan saw all of the exhibits he asked me if we were now in the 'dinosaur moo-zeum.') Surprisingly there were plenty of things that appealed to him (most of it being the state-of-the-art interactive stations sprinkled throughout the hall). One of the stations took a photo of Krischan's face, displayed it on a screen and allowed him to paint it in orange and blue and select from an assortment of Gator logos. Another allowed him to 'measure up' against a 6'6" Auburn football player (Krischan was a hair under 4'). The most interesting station were large touch-screen devices suspended from the ceiling that allowed you to revisit the legends of yesterday via historic footage, interviews and testimonials. Well, at least they *looked* interesting—between Cindy and I we have less technological know-how than most five-year olds so we were never able to navigate our way through the screen but we did manage to get an error message... on a computer screen that everyone else in the Hall didn't seem to have a problem with. I can't remember the wording on the error message, but it said something like this:

Remove your hand from the screen and walk away
before you cause any irrevocable damage to this system.
May we suggest giving your grandson a chance?

5:20 – 5:45 p.m.   A small artificial-turf playing field is located on the first floor of the Hall. Krischan couldn't wait to get to it (he could see it from both the second and third floors where we had spent the first 80 minutes). This should be fun.

Activity #1: Throw three footballs at three holes in a large net from a distance of 20 yards. Translation for a five-year old: Throw three footballs with all your might in the general direction of the man in uniform standing beside the net, using two hands if the football is too large for one hand (it most definitely was). Krischan made three crisp two-handed floaters—with all his might--to the man in uniform who took the ball each time and slammed it into each of the three holes in the net, completing the finest and perhaps only trio of alley-oops in the history of football.

Activity #2: Run shoulder-first into a blocking sled, weave through eight tackling dummies and catch a pass while falling into a large foam cushion. Translation for a five-year old: Do what is necessary to avoid the blocking sled, run straight through eight tackling dummies and dive into a large foam cushion while a perfectly-thrown pass floats over your head.

Activity #3: Kick a 20-yard field goal from a tee. Translation for a five-year old: Run towards the football and do whatever is necessary to distinguish whatever you do to it from anything you might do to a soccer ball. This one was doomed from the start. Man in uniform (to Krischan): 'Left-footed or right-footed?' Krischan: (shrugs). Man: 'Left or right?' Krischan: (still shrugging from the first time). In the end it didn't matter—left or right—because when Krischan reached the ball and made contact with his right foot (I can't say he actually 'kicked' the ball, rather he 'moved the ball with the top of his foot') the football traveled about 10 yards along the ground. Disappointed he didn't 'kick the football between the yellow poles,' I told Krischan he made a good kick but the wind got hold of it.

Activity #4: Cornhole, where the object is to toss a beanbag into a small circular hole cut into a wooden ramp from a distance of 10 yards. Krischan chose me as his opponent. We made four sets of four throws; I managed to put one into the hole in each set ('Ooooh G-Pa, you DID it!' said with the excitement I wish he'd shown Danny Wuerffel a little over an hour ago). Krischan never got one of his beanbags in the hole, but he did manage to throw a beanbag sideways, backwards, straight up, three yards and 23 yards among his 16 tosses. While my throws were a lot more consistent, Krischan's throws were a lot more creative (and dangerous to anyone in the general vicinity of the cornhole area).

5:45 – 6:00 p.m.   The last stop was the gift shop. Krischan spotted a small Florida Gator football, picked it up and asked if he could have so he could play football with his G-Pa. The price tag was hefty—as you might expect in any moo-zeum—but you might say the odds were stacked heavily in Krischan's favor. My only grandson wanted a football—his first football and a *Gator* football, no less—so he could play with his G-Pa.

My American Express had about as much of a chance as Krischan's 20-yard field goal try.

When Cindy and I attended the University of Florida we didn't have very good football teams. In fact each season ended with cries of 'wait 'til next year.'

Wait 'til next year indeed. Krischan started practicing with his small Florida Gator football today. Next year I'll wager he'll be kicking the football 'between the yellow poles.'

On behalf of both Krischan and I: Go Gators!

CHAPTER 48

Country on the Rocks

∞∞∞

Attend a Country Music Concert

At this point in my life I've come to realize there are some things I'm better off doing without. Like the metric system, 'all things science,' anything written by Fyodor Dostoyevsky and Cracker Jacks® *(Spoiler alert: Diverticulitis takes all the fun out of peanuts and popcorn).*

A few others: Trail running, tents (camping, circus, revival—what they're used for is irrelevant; I just have no use for tents), people who use 'my bad' in place of 'I'm sorry' and waiting in lines.

One more: Country music.

Don't get me wrong. In the early 1980's I made an honest effort to like country music. It was right after *Urban Cowboy* was released and long neck beer, cowboy boots and Mickey Gilley were all the rage. Although I never bought myself a ten-gallon hat *(Instant Fact: They fill up with water when it rains)* I did make a few forays into Atlanta's country music scene; namely Mama's Country Showcase and West Texas Music Club, two country music bars that were doing quite well at the time. Once I even spent eight seconds holding on for dear life on the back of one of those mechanical bulls, thanks to a potentially deadly combination of peer pressure, challenged manhood and liquid courage. I held on for the full

223

eight seconds, but I couldn't scratch my nose with my own hands for three days afterwards.

In spite of those nights on the town trying to force myself to like country music, it just never 'took.' (I did, however like *Always on My Mind* by Willie Nelson. Still do, in fact. Catchy tune sung by that distinctive/haunting voice in a Neil Young kind of way). The best word I can use to describe the sound of country music is...*Scratch that thought.* Let me just say that as far as I'm concerned, country is the metric system of the music world; that way nobody gets their feelings hurt.

So now that my quest to enjoy a wad of chewing tobacco, rope goats and feel comfortable in a pair of tight-fitting, boot-hugging blue jeans is nothing more than a distant (and by 'distant' I actually mean 'traumatizing') memory I did something I should have tried 30 years ago: I went to a country music concert.

Let me explain.

Cindy was out of town when I found out the Zac Brown Band was playing a charity concert at the Southern Ground Amphitheater (one of our favorite venues for a concert) in Fayetteville, Georgia on October 30—a 'Trick or Treat Tailgate' concert for the first 1,500 who purchased tickets. I gave Cindy a call and told her about it and she—without hesitation and despite the $100 charge for general admission ($200 for reserved seating) said she wanted to go. Her friend Jan wanted tickets for her and her husband Chuck as well.

So why did Zac Brown become 'the chosen one?' Several reasons:

- Cindy says she likes his music *('It's not really country,'* according to her).

- Cindy and I love eating at his restaurant in Senoia, the Southern Ground Social Club. The food is absolutely amazing and the employees do a great job and seem to have a lot of fun. And it shows.

- The proceeds for the concert were going to charity (and one we both support, Zac's 'passion project' Camp Southern Ground. His dream is 'that children of all abilities will have an opportunity to experience the magic of the outdoors.' The man has his head on straight, he does.

- Zac Brown is one of Cindy's customers at her Branch and Vine store in Peachtree City, which is more than likely the reason she told me his music is *'not really country.'*

- Cindy was sooo impressed with Zac and his family (wife and four daughters, each one a wee bit taller than the next) the first time they met.

- Cindy and Zac talked about selling her products (oil and vinegar) at the Southern Ground Social Club, and once he reads the rave review I'm about to write it will be a done deal *(right, Zac?)*.

So on the eve of Halloween the four of us took our lawn chairs to Zac's amphitheater where we dined on Zac's food (his restaurant had a booth), listened to Zac and his band and contributed money towards Zac's passion project *(Zac should be having his attorneys draw up an agreement with Branch and Vine any second now)*.

The opening band was…well, let's just say they played for about 45 minutes while we stood in line to order our food. I can't vouch for the quality of the band, but I can tell you my ears didn't start bleeding so I took that as a good sign.

The Zac Brown Band took the stage around 8 p.m. With the exception of our party of four, it seemed everyone else in the amphitheater knew the first couple of songs by heart. They were all standing, singing and clapping while the four of us were sitting, shivering *(the amphitheater is an outdoor venue, and the temperature was 48 degrees…and falling)* and acclimating ourselves to the weather as well as the music of Zac Brown. *(I tried to condition myself a few days prior to the concert by listening to a couple of Zac's* music videos; as was the case 30 years ago, this particular experiment didn't 'take' either.)

But then something amazing happened. Zac talked about his early exposure to classic rock and one of his all-time favorite albums, *Dark Side of the Moon*, which led to his cover version of *Comfortably Numb*. OK, now we're on to something.

Next? Metallica's *Enter Sandman*. The best part of the song was when five *(five!)* guitars were all wailing at the same time *(and no I didn't include you, Mister Fiddle Guy because I don't even consider Charlie Daniels when I'm counting guitars)* and I suddenly realized I was no longer chilly but rather about to break out in a sweat. *This band was bringing the heat!*

A few more country songs followed *(I took a breather and sat in my lawn chair)*—one sounded sort of Boz Scaggs-ish that as far as I'm concerned is never a bad thing—before Zac's version of the Marshall Tucker Band's *Can't You See* filled the cool October air. The four of us were back on our feet, joining the other 1,496 in attendance.

Then the finale, a song 'written by a genius on so many levels' as Zac said an instant before the first cords of *Bohemian Rhapsody* were struck. Zac and his band 'done good' with Freddie Mercury's opus, a long song that ended way too soon…at least as far as I was concerned. I don't think I was alone in that thought.

Zac ended the evening by thanking everyone for supporting the band and their music, the community and most importantly Camp Southern Ground.

Did you ever hear the phrase 'expect the worse and hope for the best?' Yeah, it was that kind of a night. Especially for someone who wants the name of his music trivia team to be 'No Country for Old Man.'

Cindy was right about Zac Brown: He's a really good guy who believes in and tries to do all the right things. That makes it easy to support him in his endeavors. While I may not be rushing out to buy a Zac Brown CD anytime soon, I'll continue to patronize his restaurant and look forward to the grand opening of his passion project.

As for the night, I can honestly say that it was the best country music concert I've ever attended.

Swear to God.

CHAPTER 49

Color My World
(Orange and Blue)

Renew my Marriage Vows

My wife Cindy drove down to Florida with her friend Jan for a 'girl's weekend' a couple of months ago. History shows that while the cat's away this mouse will play. Cindy—no slouch when it comes to history-knows this but she went anyway.

For this particular mouse, 'play' means tackling some major project that I can complete—my own way without any outside influence, interference or interruptions--before the cat returns. For example rearranging the furniture in every single room in the house...or replacing the wooden fencing in the backyard with white vinyl...or painting the walls of the Florida Gator room (what else?) orange and blue. Actually that last one never happened because whenever Cindy leaves for an extended period of time she specifically tells me NOT to paint any of the rooms orange and blue...which sort of leaves the door open for me to paint the OUTSIDE of the house the color (or colors, as the case may be) of my choice.

Since we're barely three months into our new home, I felt it was a little premature to paint the outside of the house. Therefore I had to come up with a new project for the seven days Cindy would be gone. Keeping my grandson for the weekend and working my regular job Monday through Friday made it difficult to tackle anything significant. So I had to ask myself: *What to do?...*

Then I recalled Cindy making a comment in the spring about renewing our marriage vows. If I could make that happen, I thought, that would be a surprise she could live with. If I could make that happen, I thought, it could earn me a lifetime of brownie points; perhaps one day leading to permission to paint a room orange and blue. If I could make that happen without her knowing it UNTIL it happened, I thought, she may very well rip me a new one.

Carefully weighing all of these factors I deemed it worthy of my undertaking and started planning the moment she and Jan drove down the driveway and headed south to Destin. In fact by the time they crossed the Georgia-Florida state line a few hours later I had everything orchestrated in my head as to how I was going to pull off this most excellent surprise. The first thing was to make sure everyone on my marriage vow renewal ceremony guest list was available:

- My sister Hope and her boyfriend already had plans to visit. They would be arriving on a Friday (Halloween) and the annual Florida-Georgia football game would be played the following day. Seriously, could there possibly be a better cover for a surprise marriage vow renewal ceremony than a local rendition of the World's Largest Outdoor Cocktail Party, as the Florida-Georgia game is known?

- I sent an Email to Steve and Becky Clark to see if they would be available the afternoon of the football game. Steve is one of the pastors of our church (and the first person we met when we started going there over nine years ago) and Becky (Steve's wife) is an organist/vocalist with our church band. Karma is in my favor: They're available.

- I sent an invitation to our Cindy's brothers (Don and Robert) and their wives to spend the weekend with us—sort of a 'house welcoming' (as far as Cindy was concerned, anyway) but primarily to be there for the ceremony. After all, they—as well as my sister Hope, were in attendance at our wedding over 37 years ago. Good news: They can both attend and Robert's wife Mary Lane, who was also at our wedding, would be coming as well.

- I invited our close friends and with the exception of Cindy's business partner and her husband (daughter's engagement party trumps business partner's marriage vow renewal ceremony), I had enough commitments to move on to the next step.

Now for the choreography (you can call me Bob Fosse):

- I met with the Clarks to go over the game plan. As Becky had been reading Part 1 of my quasibiography, *Buy the Book* she was very cognizant of the fact my blood runs orange and blue. Becky, with a son-in-law at the University of Georgia would be my perfect foil. Presto: Instant rivalry. Becky and I started trash-talking one another via Email (I must admit, she held her own and I found that very cool because I've always thought I graduated magna cum laude in trash talk) and I would share our exchanges with Cindy. Ultimately I'd invite Becky (and Steve) to watch the game with us so we could settle our fabricated rivalry once and for all. As for their role in the surprise: Steve would conduct the ceremony at the conclusion of the game, and Becky and her organ would provide the musical accompaniment. How to explain Becky showing up with her organ in tow? I would tell Cindy that Becky and I made a wager: Becky would play the alma mater of the winning team at the end of the game.

- When Cindy returned from Florida I told her about her brothers coming up to spend the weekend with us while my sister was in town. Believe it or not, convincing her that her brothers were coming proved to be more difficult than selling the idea of Becky and Steve, our fabricated rivalry and the presence of Becky's traveling organ.

- After the shock of having a house full of company for the weekend started to fade, I told Cindy I invited our close friends to come over for dinner and drinks and to enjoy the game with all of us. What Cindy actually heard me say was 'we have less than a month to get our new house presentable, make three of the guest rooms totally functional, put the yard in order and prepare menus for the weekend for a whole lot more than just the two of us.' We spent the next four weeks doing exactly that. OK, so maybe I'm no Bob Fosse after all.

But here's the cool thing: Everything came together over the next four weeks and Cindy was totally sold on the idea that it was simply friends, family, dinner, drinks and the Florida-Georgia game. The house came together, the yard was taken care of and the menus were compiled. Cindy had no reason or inclination to suspect anything else was on the agenda.

On the day of the game, Cindy left to work at her store wearing a hat. I knew right then and that she had no idea anything was amiss because there is no way in the world she would want to renew her marriage views wearing a hat. But it was a Florida Gator hat so in lieu of the day's itinerary I found it totally appropriate. In time—15, 20 years or so—she probably will as well.

The game would kick off at 3:30, so guests started arriving between 3:00 and 5:00. Becky and Steve would arrive a bit later as she had a 'gig' with her band that afternoon and they would be dropping by afterwards. Cindy and Jan spent a good bit of the afternoon fixing appetizers, cooking chili (I was given the more difficult job of putting all of the drinks on ice—those bags of ice are *heavy*) and cursing me under their breath.

The game turned out better than I could have ever imagined. The Gators—easily two touchdown underdogs—upset the Bulldogs 38-20 in a game that wasn't nearly as close as the score indicates (more on the game in the addendum to follow). Once the game was over I told everyone of the 'bet' and asked everyone to listen as Becky played the alma mater of the University of Florida

With all eyes on Becky, she began playing Chicago's *Color My World*, one of the songs Cindy and I considered 'ours' when we started dating over 40 years ago that was also the theme of our senior prom. I had earlier told everyone that once Cindy heard the first few notes of the song she would know I was up to something.

I was wrong. Becky kept playing, sang the entire song and I could tell by the look on Cindy's face she was none the wiser (Cindy told me later she thought Becky was 'warming up' before playing the alma mater). Then Steve walked to the front of the room and asked Cindy and I to join him in front of the fireplace.

That's when Cindy finally realized there would be no alma mater. *That's* when Cindy realized I was up to something. *That's* when Cindy knew she wanted to wring my neck for letting her wear a hat in what was about to transpire.

Steve then delivered the most eloquent, sincere and heart-felt ceremony I could have ever hoped for while Becky softly played the songs I requested—songs that have special meaning for Cindy and I. Bread's *If* and *I Wanna Make it with You* and Todd Rundgren's *Hello It's Me*. Steve interacted with friends and family by asking who was at our wedding (Hope, Don, Robert and Mary Lane all raised their hands) and if they remembered anything about what happened that night. Once it was established that a bad storm had passed through Atlantic Beach, the power in the church had gone out and we were married by candlelight, the glo-sticks everyone had in their hands made a lot more sense. Naturally I had all the lights in the house turned off to re-enact that night (the glo-sticks providing the only semblance of light) and noticed Steve was having trouble reading his notes.

I turned on a lamp so he could read portions of a letter I wrote to Cindy on our anniversary a little over four months ago. It sounded amazing, if I do say so myself—perhaps because it actually was incredibly well-written, perhaps because it was so eloquently spoken by Steve, most likely because of the beer I drank earlier in the evening—it was hard to believe I wrote it. Then he asked Cindy if there was anything she wanted to say to *me*.

She started by mentioning my bachelor party. '*Uh oh,*' my thought balloon whispered to me. With good reason: The only thing I remember about my bachelor party is that my best man Stan rolled what he called the 'bachelor special' and then we went for a ride in Stan's car, stopped at a traffic light and woke up almost three hours later. What Cindy remembers is that my sister dropped by and tried to talk me out of getting married (she didn't want me to live in Florida since she and my parents were in Virginia) in the middle of my bachelor party (Stan and I apparently were busy polishing off the 'bachelor special' at the time because I have no recollection of seeing her that night). Hope had the best retort (in a world where humor trumps reality): '*What did I know? I was only seven!*'

Back to reality, because next on the itinerary was The Moment of Truth. Steve asked us to hold one another's hands and…well, you know what came next. Two 'I do's' and a kiss later and it was over. Steve asked if anyone had anything they would like to say, and Cindy's brothers both wished us all the best in our marriage and our new home.

Once Steve concluded the ceremony Cindy leaned towards me and whispered in my ear the most romantic thing she said all night:

How could you let me wear a hat on a night like this?

I may have to hit the 'pause' button on that second honeymoon.

ADDENDUM
Karma comes in Colors

I've been watching Florida Gator football for over 40 years and I'll go on record as saying—IMHO—this year's team is the worst I've ever seen. Somehow the Gators won three of their first four games this season (a one-point win over hapless Tennessee, a triple-overtime win over even more hapless Kentucky and a gazillion point win over Podunk U) to go with a three-touchdown loss to Alabama. Then in their fifth game they had the opportunity to beat a respectable LSU team. That is up until the moment the senior Gator tight end—so alone in the end zone that the closest person in an LSU jersey was sitting in the fourth row—dropped a pass that every other person in the stadium wearing a Gator jersey (to include the five women sitting in the Zeta Tau Alpha block in town for their 50-year reunion weekend, all wearing identical Tim Tebow #15 jerseys) would have caught.

The following Saturday—homecoming at the University of Florida, no less—Missouri came to town and soundly whipped the orange and blue in what (again, IMHO) undoubtedly was the absolute worst game ever played by a Gator team in the Swamp (the Gators' home field).

So with the crowd chanting 'Fire Muschamp' (Muschamp being the Gator Head Coach) at the end of the game and the Gators sporting a record of three wins and three losses, it didn't look good as they prepared for their annual rivalry game against the Georgia Bulldogs—sporting a record of 6-1 and a Top Ten ranking—the following Saturday. *(This would be the same Saturday I chose to renew our marriage vows, in case you lost track.)* Georgia was easily a two-touchdown favorite to win the game. Personally I thought the odds makers were taking it easy on the Gators because I thought we had an excellent chance of losing by as many as four touchdowns or more. Like we did against Missouri, whom Georgia had beaten soundly earlier in the season.

So to say that I had no expectations of a good outcome for the orange and blue against Georgia would be an understatement. Even the Georgia fans weren't the same during the week leading up to the game. I've always known them to be cocky the week of the Florida-Georgia game. This year they were more in the neighborhood of confident, with just a slight touch of their usual cockiness. 'Cockfident,' you might call it.

The morning of the game I placed a few pieces of my Gator memorabilia around the television set to generate some good karma. A University of Florida helmet, a framed print of an alligator chasing a bulldog (signed by former Gator/Heisman Trophy winner Danny Wuerffel) and the framed newspaper clipping from the 2008 Florida-Georgia game (A 49-10 Gator victory. The headline: *'Dogs Pounded.'*). Then I prayed. A lot.

You'll never guess what happened next. Georgia easily scored the first touchdown *(on second thought you probably did guess that)* and jumped out to a 7-0 lead. But then *(this is what you couldn't possibly have guessed)* the Gators scored the NEXT THIRTY-ONE POINTS! When the dust settled Florida had a 38-20 victory and Georgia (once again, the dogs were pounded) left the stadium wondering how they could surrender 190 rushing yards to—not one but TWO—Gator running backs.

I took the victory as an omen that what I was about to do—renew my marriage vows with my high school sweetheart and fellow Florida Gator— was the right thing to do.

At our wedding we both wore white. Today? Orange and blue.

As I said earlier: Karma.

Postscript: The Gators had a legitimate chance at beating Florida State in the final game of the regular season. Sporting a 9 – 0 lead and with the ball on FSU's eight-yard line the Gator quarterback threw a perfect pass to the senior tight end (yes, the same senior tight end mentioned in the LSU game) who promptly allowed the football to bounce off his shoulder pads and into the hands of an FSU defender who returned it over 90 yards for a touchdown. It changed the game in a instant: What could have been a 16 – 0 Gator lead resulted in a 9 – 7 Gator lead, but the momentum had clearly shifted over to the Seminoles who went on to win the game and complete their second consecutive undefeated season. The Gators finished their season in search of a new head coach…not to mention a tight end that knows how to catch a football.

CHAPTER 50

Age Gracefully

—⚬⚬⚬—

Run 60 Miles for my 60th Birthday (maybe more)

It started over 20 years ago. On my 40th birthday I ran 40 miles. On my 45th birthday I ran 45 miles. This went on for another decade until I decided that 55 miles on my 55th birthday was a good place to call a truce—on behalf of my abused body--between running my age in miles every five years. Or at least 'convert' to kilometers on my 60th birthday (that would mean running 37.2 miles for anyone not fluent in metric).

As I've come to learn, time has a way of sneaking up on you. I'll be 60 this December and it was time to make a decision. It took all of 60 seconds:

I wanted to run 60 miles; kilometers are for wimps (sorry, Europe).

The first thing I needed was an accomplice. *What's that, Sarah? You just ran your first 100-miler this summer, you're hungry for more and all I have to do is say 'when?' Give me a couple of dates that work for you and I'll see which days I have available and we'll go from there.*

Once Sarah and I agreed that Sunday, November 16 would work for both of us I got an Email with the volunteer schedule for church. My wife Cindy and I were scheduled to work at Grand Central (the information counter) on November 16. I asked Kathi the scheduler to swap me out with someone on November 23 and asked that she not tell Cindy about my plans to run 60 miles on the 16th.

So what happens next? Cindy comes home one evening and says she saw a revised Grand Central schedule and that I was no longer scheduled to work with her on the 16th. I said I asked Kathi to schedule me for the 23rd as I had something to do on the 16th.

Cindy: 'Kathi said you were running a race. Are you going out of town?'

Me: 'No. I'll be here.'

Cindy: 'Are you going to be running?'

Me: 'Yes.'

Cindy: 'And it's going to take most of the day?'

Me: 'Yes.'

Cindy: 'Well, it's not your birthday.'

Me: 'But it's *almost* my birthday.'

Cindy: 'Oh Lord, please don't tell me you're running 60 miles.'

Me: 'OK, I won't.'

(Insert sound of lead balloon hitting the ground)

Cindy knows me all too well. I think in her heart she knew 60 miles was inevitable, although she was probably hoping and praying I would convert to the metric system once I reached decade # 6.

As the date drew nearer the usual suspects lined up to run some of the miles with me. Al, Susan, Val, Eric, Sarah and my son Josh said they'd be out to give me the best birthday gift they could possibly offer: Themselves.

I laid out a flat (well, at least it seemed flat when I drove it in my truck), shaded 2 ½ mile route starting and finishing in downtown Haralson (Population zero, although it is a very familiar locale to anyone who watches the opening credits to *The Walking Dead*). The plan was to run the loop 24 times counterclockwise beginning at 6 a.m. My friends could join me any time throughout the day. Their instructions: Look for my blue Gator truck in deserted, downtown Haralson and wait—I'll be coming by about every 27 minutes for the first 35 miles or so, but after that all bets were off. I hoped to finish up around 6 p.m. if everything went according to plan.

Sarah and Josh started with me at (officially) 6:02 a.m. Josh, getting a little exposure to an ultrarunning endeavor, studied the assorted food and drink I loaded on the back of the truck: Gatorade, water, soda, chocolate milk, ginger snaps and pretzels—all things I would soon be sick of and wouldn't eat or drink for weeks after today. We used a flashlight for the first loop as we took note of the solitude and the incredibly great weather we were blessed with (40 degrees, slight breeze, overcast). Josh ran 10 miles and then headed home as he was going to church with Cindy. I made note that Josh stopped to answer Nature's Call about every three miles, lending more support to the 'apple not falling far from the tree' theory. Sarah held on for 25 miles before calling it a day, but by that time Eric had shown up wanting to run 20 miles so it looked like I'd have company for at least the first 45 miles of my run.

Now would be a good time to interject what didn't happen during the course of the day:

- I didn't trip and fall.
- I didn't have to stop to answer Nature's *Other* Call.
- I didn't change clothes (although I did remove my jacket after the first loop).
- I didn't change shoes.
- I didn't cuss (although Eric said I exhaled the word 'sh*t' every other breath).

- I didn't have any close encounters with mean dogs or hostile Haralsonians.
- I didn't quit. (Wanted to, but didn't. More on that shortly.)

Al and Susan showed up for their 10 miles shortly after Eric started running with me. Once Eric completed his 20 miles and called it a day, I still had six more ibuprofen remaining before my run was complete. (Let me explain: I counted off 24 ibuprofen—one for each of the laps I needed to run—and placed them on the right side of the back bumper on the truck. After each lap I would move one ibuprofen to the left side of the bumper; once all 24 had made it from one side to the other I would be finished. My only concern was if someone showed up while I was in the middle of a loop, consumed a couple of the ibuprofen and forget which pile they took them from.)

I ran briskly for the next three laps once Eric left (no one was with me, so yes, I RAN BRISKLY FOR THE NEXT THREE LAPS). Towards the end of my 21st lap I heard a car approaching me from behind: It was Val. She was finished showing houses for the day and could go home (she lives about three miles away) and change into her running attire if I wanted company for the final three laps. If she only knew what was running through my head during that 21st lap (52 ½ miles isn't bad, is it? Who could fault me if I stopped? Etc., etc.) she wouldn't have needed to ask.

Fifteen minutes later she returned and the two of us ran, walked, reminisced (Val and I have been friends so long that she was by my side when I ran my 40th mile on my 40th birthday, and I was by her side three weeks later when she ran her 35th mile on her 35th birthday) and laughed—yes, *LAUGHED*—until the last three ibuprofen made it to the left side of the bumper.

I looked at my watch when we finished: 6:12 p.m. We shared a couple of beers I had hidden in the cooler beneath the two 64-ounce bottles of Gatorade and 20 pounds of ice. Pitch black evening (you couldn't see the stars for the cloud cover), total silence, deserted town of Haralson— boarded up buildings everywhere—and two old friends sharing a beer after doing what they love doing most. Val hit the nail on the head when she referred to it as 'surreal,' because it most certainly was.

I took the following day as a vacation day from work. After all, I'm not a 52-or-53-year-old kid anymore (and the mere fact that I refer to someone 52 or 53 as a 'kid' sort of tells you something about me) and I knew I'd need the day to recover.

That next morning—after my two cups of coffee, of course—I took a personal inventory of which parts of my body hurt. Here's a short list:

- Everything.

Al has been encouraging me for years—starting about the time I was still a 52-or-52-year-old kid—that I should learn to cut back my mileage, stop running so hard and age gracefully. Now that I've gotten this 60-miler out of my system I'm ready to do just that.

Note to Val: Thanks for pulling me through those last three loops. I don't think I could have done them without you. Honest in'jun. I'm sorry I won't be in town in a few weeks for your birthday. That is, unless you're ready to convert to kilometers. Then we'll talk.

Postscript: Two weeks later—on Sunday, November 30, 2014—I ran. The day was the 36-year anniversary of the day I started a streak of running every day. Two weeks after that I ran the Tallahassee Ultra Distance Classic 50K… and ran 10 additional kilometers to bookend my birthday run: 60 miles on the front and 60 kilometers on the back. What the heck: I did the same thing when I turned 40 and 50. I promise not to do it again at 70.

Post-Postscript: Four weeks later I ran the Jacksonville Marathon, thereby giving me a marathon finish in five decades (20's, 30's, 40's, 50's and now 60's). My friend Al turns 70 next May. He also has run a marathon in five decades. The ball is now in his court.

SOLO PERFORMANCES

———— ∞ ————

There are things I've done that I doubt anyone else has had the pleasure, misfortune or personal idiosyncrasies to have on their personal inventory of life accomplishments

Ladies and gentlemen, things I may be the only person in the world who has ever done:

- Attend three Doobie Brothers concert and fall asleep during each one. The first two were in the early '70's, so I actually 'passed out' rather than fell asleep thanks to a preconcert routine of beer and screwdrivers. The third one was in 2003—about 30 years later-- and there was no doubt I was simply asleep. I was almost 50 and it was after 10:00 p.m.

- Deliver an impromptu eulogy. For a man I'd never met. Long story; short eulogy.

- I played golf as a teenager at the Mayport (Florida) Naval Station Golf Course. There were three par-three holes. Once in a tournament I played those three holes in a cumulative five strokes. I'll leave the math to you.

- I have this habit of crushing aluminum cans with my right hand once I finish drinking whatever was inside. I do this for two reasons: (1) If anyone wonders who left an empty aluminum can on the counter, on the table, etc. and it wasn't crushed, they'll know it wasn't me, and (2) as a reminder to myself that I've finished drinking it (please reference earlier comment regarding sleeping through *China Grove, Long Train Running, etc.*).

• Quit drinking tequila after tasting it for the first time in the fall of 1974. Why? Simple math, actually. First time = 15 shots.

• Drink an entire bottle of Manischewitz Blackberry Wine right before taking a physical examination. You see, I knew the nurse would be drawing blood from my arm and I have this incredible fear of needles… Incidentally, the results indicated an extraordinarily high sugar level in my blood. Go figure.

• Survive a root canal without any anesthetic. You see, I knew the dentist would be injecting Novocain in my gums and I have this incredible fear of needles… *(Please note: If you want to get an idea what it felt like, chew on a large piece of aluminum foil and be sure it comes in lots of contact with every last one of your teeth with fillings. Then stab a fork in your gums.)*

• Catch someone else's vomit in their bare hands. Two family members from two generations in the same house in virtually the same spot: My son Justin (circa: 1990) and *his* son Krischan (circa: so recent I can still envision if not *smell* it in the palms of my hands!).

• Average less than six hours of sleep daily for 35 years. My eighth book was published in September. It's called *The Edge of Exhaustion* and chronicles my quest for a personal 'Grand Slam' of the Major Ultras: The JFK 50, the Badwater Ultramarathon, Western States and the Comrades Marathon. It will help explain things, like how I managed to run as many miles as I did while maintaining a full time job and raising two boys, as well as why I can't stay awake through an entire Doobie Brothers concert.

• Begin every day with a run. Focus on the words 'begin' and 'every day.' Since November 30, 1978 to be exact. Now focus on 'run' and realize the word is interchangeable with jog, walk, stumble, crawl and on occasion, drag my sorry a**.

- Have five felines stick to them like glue. This happens every time I'm away from home for a couple of days. Our cats must really miss the hand that feeds them, the lap that comforts them and the person who rakes their litter boxes every ~~stinking~~ single morning. Amendment: I may be the only person with five felines sticking to them like clue that isn't (a) a female or (b) a lion tamer.

- Write every day for an entire year. The year was 2013. You can find everything I wrote in *My Life: Everything but BUY THE BOOK* (Parts 1 and 2). Three hundred and sixty-five chapters in all: One chapter written on each day of the year. If I had to do it all over again I might have divided everything into four books rather than two since there were almost as many pages (1,040) in them as there are in *War and Peace* (1,296). However, if you are looking for more of the backstory behind anything you've read in this story, rest assured you'll never find it in anything Tolstoy ever wrote.

- Meet Alice Cooper. OK, I realize lots of people have met Alice Cooper but I wanted to make sure everyone knew I MET ALICE COOPER! How cool is that?!?

- Sing Billy Joel's *Just the Way You Are* and getting all the lyrics right. While hammered. Company Christmas party 1983, to be exact. One year later I sang the Commodores *Still*. Messed up on a few lyrics on that one but it was my own damn fault: I tried singing it sober.

- Discover the Algorithm for Measuring Dead Weight (AMDW). This is the numerical representation for calculating how much heavier it is to lift a *sleeping* child than one who is awake. I realized this equation through repeated lifts when Krischan spent time with Cindy and I after turning five years old. Krischan weighed in at 52 pounds at the time. When he ran and jumped into my arms, it was a 'true' 52 pounds. However, when he fell asleep in the car on the drive home from wherever that particular day took us, he easily weighed in at 80 pounds. I know this to be true because after I got Krischan safely into the house and on the couch I went to the garage and played around with the weights on the barbells until the weight I was lifting felt *exactly* how it felt when I lifted Krischan out of the back seat. So let the record show the AMDW as:

$$X + X\,(.54) = Y$$

(X is the weight of the awakened child and Y
is the weight of the sleeping child)

So husbands, the next time you attempt to lift your sleeping 140-pound wife off the couch and carry her upstairs to bed, remember you're essentially trying to lift a 216-pound weight.

- Discover (I'm in a 'discovery-kind-of-mood') the Absolute Principle of Allowable Facebook Posts (APAFP). This principle is to discourage those who tend to promote their personal views of matters—religion, politics, gun control, abortions—via Facebook posts. Everyone knows the old adage 'opinions are like a**holes; everybody has one,' right? Well, let's take it a step further to explain the APAFP:

    *Everyone has an a**hole, but you don't see them
    posting pictures of it on Facebook.*

THE CALIPARI LIST

———— ∞ ————

The Calipari List is a compilation of things I've done only one time in my life...and have absolutely no plans to do again. You know, my 'one and dones.'

The list is named after current University of Kentucky basketball coach John Calipari, who makes a living recruiting the top freshman in the country only to play one season of college basketball for him, display their prowess in front of the entire nation and leave for the NBA well before they turn 20.

You should also know the list is named after John Calipari not as a flattering gesture, but rather as a means to express my reprehension for what he has done to the game of college basketball.

With that being said, here is my Calipari List; things I've only done once and vow to never do again:

- Wear sunglasses at night. I tried it once. What a stupid idea: I couldn't see sh*t. If you see someone wearing sunglasses at night you have my blessing to tell them they look stupid. Footnote: I have never worn sunglasses inside, since I've never been in a house with a glass roof on a sunny day. I doubt anyone else has either, so if you see someone wearing sunglasses inside, tell them they look stupid also.

- Watch *Blade Runner*. Rotten tomatoes calls it 'a visually remarkable, achingly human sci-fi masterpiece.' I call it a master piece as well; a master piece of sh*t.

- Pierce an ear. Long story, but here's the short version: Happy hour + too much 'happy' + well-timed dare + very sharp needle + one solitary ice cube = pierced ear.

- Eat octopus. Cindy and I had dinner at Burt's Place (owned by Burt Reynolds) on our honeymoon. Cindy ordered a fancy dish--Neptune's Pasta, maybe--and offered me a bite. I took one bite and thought I detected a piece of seafood in the sauce, perhaps from the shellfish family. WRONG! Octopus tentacle. Further inspection of Cindy's dinner revealed all kinds of tentacles covered in suction cups (not the scientific term for them, but you know what I mean) sticking out of the plate of pasta. Miraculously we didn't turn Burt's Place into a modern-day vomitorium.

- Chew chewing tobacco. If only I had stopped at 'chew.' If only the person who gave me the chewing tobacco had TOLD me to stop at 'chew.' At least it was wintergreen flavored (I've always liked wintergreen) and I didn't turn the softball field we were playing on at the time into a modern-day vomitorium.

- Ingest a flower. It was the night I became a Cardinal Puff at the local bar during my sophomore year in college. It only took me two pitchers of beer to achieve that distinction, quite the accomplishment for someone who hadn't reached their 20th birthday. So I ate a flower to celebrate. If I would have had a couple of dollars I would have bought a pizza, but like I said, I was a sophomore in college. I spent all my money on beer.

- Make a hole-in-one. April 8, 1972. Mayport Naval Station Golf Course. I fancied myself as a pretty good golfer at the time, keeping my scores in the low 70's most of the time. One year later--TO THE DAY--I saw my dad make a hole-in-one on the very same golf course. My dad struggled to break 100. That was the day I realized making a hole-in-one had nothing to do with being good.

- Travel to South Africa. I flew for 20 hours to run a race from Durban to Johannesburg. I was robbed at knifepoint in Durban a mere 12 hours before the start of the race. Three hours later I discovered the local police didn't give a rat's ass about the lives of tourists in their country. After a sleepless night I managed to finish the hilly-as-hell 54-mile race, more a testament to the anger I felt towards South Africa than a tribute to the condition I was in at the time. I vowed never to return: YOU try sitting in an airplane for 20 hours sometime.

- Use the word 'ingest' when I could have (and most likely *should* have) used 'ate.'

100 Things I've Never Done
(or don't remember doing if I did)

1. Win the Presidential Medal of Honor (I did, however earn the Citizenship merit badge in Boy Scouts. Let's call it 'even.').

2. Play a video game more advanced than Space Invaders (the original version, circa mid 1970's).

3. Run for public office (the only time I ever ran for anything was President of my 7th grade class at Moanalua Intermediate School; I lost).

4. Appear on Broadway.

5. Break a leg (literally or, having never been on Broadway, figuratively).

6. Solve a Rubik's Cube (excluding the beginner's version that I bought in solid blue).

7. Become a Rhodes Scholar (although I did win the second grade Spelling Bee at the American School of the Hague in 1963—'b-o-u-n-t-i-f-u-l').

8. Bowl a perfect game (but ask me about my hole-in-one anytime).

9. Attend a boxing match.

10. Own a pet tarantula (although I had a boa constrictor named 'Alice' my freshman year in college).

11. See *Rocky Horror Picture Show, This is Spinal Tap* or *Young Frankenstein* (so sue me).

12. Meet the Beatles (although I did see Paul McCartney in concert in Atlanta once and became pals with Julian Lennon on a chance meeting at a deli in New York City in 1985 when *Too Late for Goodbyes* was on the Top 40 Charts (Me: '*Love your song!*' Julian: '*Who the hell are you?*').

13. Get the hell out of Dodge (I've never even been to Dodge).

14. Successfully give something up for the entire 40 days of Lent although this year I gave up Diet Coke until the Caffeine Headache from Hell came late on the second day and I surrendered.

15. Appear on *Saturday Night Live* (although I've been to the diner the famous '*Cheeseburger cheeseburger cheeseburger*' sketches were based on. Twice. It's in Chicago, if you're interested.

16. Watch an episode of *Downton Abbey* (nor do I *know* anyone who has ever seen an episode of *Downton Abbey*).

17. Understand a single thing about chemistry.

18. Parachute, paraglide or parasail.

19. Play poker (not even strip poker; in high school I simplified and played strip *war*).

20. Understand the rules of poker (Duh!).

21. Win the lottery.

22. Watch all 238 minutes of Gone with the Wind from start to finish in one sitting.

23. Understand what anyone sees in post-NFL Michael Strahan.

24. Try out for a television game show (but I'm pretty good playing at home but no doubt would totally suck in front of a studio audience).

25. Appreciate the humor of Monty Python.

26. Roast chestnuts on an open fire.

27. Have Sex on the Beach (the mixed drink).

28. Kick myself in the a** for not coming up with the idea for *The Walking Dead*.

29. Shoot a gun while drinking a beer.

30. Shoot a gun at a beer can.

31. Shotgun a beer.

32. Bring up religion or politics in conversation (if we've ever spoken, you're welcome).

33. Eat a Thin Mint Girl Scout cookie.

34. Read anyone's lips (unless they're saying 'vacuum' ever so slowly).

35. Willingly or knowingly eat a Jalapeno pepper.

36. Read an entire issue of *Playboy* magazine.

37. Go over the river and through the woods to get to my grandmother's house.

38. Drink coffee after dinner (lunch either, for that matter).

39. Travel to South America, Asia or the Soviet Union (of the three there's only one I would even consider…).

40. Limbo.

41. Start a fire/burn an ant with a magnifying glass.

42. Help tear down a goal post after a big win. (After further review, I DID do that. In 1984. Florida – 27, Georgia – 0.)

43. Turn down an opportunity to take a pot shot at the University of Georgia (reference #42 above).

44. Engage in a duel (the proximity of this to #42 is merely a coincidence).

45. Throw an honest-to-goodness knuckleball.

46. Hit an honest-to-goodness knuckleball.

47. Understand the physics behind an honest-to-goodness knuckleball.

48. Understand physics period.

49. Lose well.

50. Siphon gas.

51. Accept the 'i' before 'e' except after 'c' rule (thanks to you, neighbor).

52. Learn the metric system (although I'm quite adept at ordering a pint).

53. Say anything nice about Bobby Petrino (seriously now, has *anyone?*).

54. Fear fear itself (there has always been a reason).

55. Call a time out (as much as I would like to on a daily basis).

56. Eat an elephant one bite at a time.

57. Refrain from laughing when there's a fart on television.

58. Comprehend how Milli Vanilli got away with it for so long.

59. Speak a foreign language (but I can count to 10 in French, Dutch and German; the numbers will be in order but the language may vary from one number to the next).

60. Pitch a tent because it was something I absolutely *wanted* to do.

61. Land a triple gainer from the high dive.

62. Land a double gainer from the high dive.

63. Attempt a triple gainer or a double gainer from the high dive (certainly you didn't confuse me with Greg Louganis, did you?).

64. Sculpt.

65. Meet a man from Nantucket.

66. Intentionally make any type of physical contact with a cockroach.

67. Understand what Sting considers to be 'tantric sex.'

68. Have anything bad to say about Tim Tebow.

69. Get a tattoo.

70. Distinguish one fireworks display from another (I guess they're like snowflakes; they're all inherently different but look exactly the same).

71. Plunge to a new low (because consistency is my game).

72. Drop down and give anyone 10 (even 5 would be a push).

73. Watch an entire episode of *American Idol, The Voice* or *Dancing with the Stars* (and darn proud of it).

74. Be late to the party (I'm always on time and yes it's a curse but I've learned to live with it and in a perfect world everyone else would be on time as well but sadly I realize that is not the case just as it will always be expected of some people to compose ridiculously long run-on sentences that lose a reader's interest by the time the sentence reaches its inevitable conclusion. Amen.).

75. Have this thought: 'Gee; today would be a good day to go to the opera.'

76. Go to the opera.

77. Be the class valid Victorian. I mean valedictorian.

78. Catch a break.

79. Wish I were a professional soccer player.

80. Wish I were an Oscar Mayer wiener (even as a boy...).

81. Remember how much is 'fourscore and seven years.'

82. Throw a 90-mile an hour fastball (80-mile an hour neither; actually, anything over 55. Yes, I have never thrown over the legal speed limit.).

83. Make sense of it all.

84. Sing *Bohemian Rhapsody* in its entirety sitting in the back seat of a police car like that drunk guy did (if you get a chance, YouTube it sometime).

85. Party all the time (Eddie Murphy might be able to; probably because he's Gumby, dammit!).

86. Find what I'm looking for.

87. Realize I lost it in the first place.

88. Avoid sushi, particularly the round ones that look like the butt of a tiny dog.

89. Roll through a stop sign.

90. *(continued from #89 above)* At more than three miles an hour.

91. Say, hear or think of 'Land Shark' or 'Candy Gram' without laughing inside.

92. Give a second thought to teaching the world to sing in perfect harmony; I wouldn't know where to start.

93. Substitute 'my bad' for 'I'm sorry.'

94. Crave chocolate.

95. Trip and fall gracefully (violently perhaps, but definitely not gracefully—I present the scar from 13 stitches to the chin as People's Exhibit #1).

96. Disappear (except for the time I played hide-and-seek with my grandson and jumped in the bathtub and hid behind the shower curtain because on that day I freakin' vanished!).

97. Trust a groundhog from Pennsylvania for a weather forecast, regardless of the date.

98. Inhale (Seriously; the thought of having any black death inside my lungs frightens me!)

99. Successfully drive in reverse with a trailer hitched to the back...except when I drive to Jackknife City that is right across town from Whatwereyouthinking Town.

100. Run 135 miles across Death Valley in 130+ degree heat. (I'm lying; I totally did that.)

LAST CALL AT WAKULLA

————⊱⊰————

From my experience I've known runners to be creatures of habit. They find a brand of running shoes that provide the comfort and support they need and use them exclusively if not religiously. They blaze a favorite trail known only to them and run it again and again until they're able to know what time it is simply by realizing where they are on the route at any given time. They discover a drink or a snack—sometimes both that has served them well during their runs and refuse to try anything else.

And if that runner is anything like me, they find a race they really enjoy and die a thousand deaths when that race is no more.

The first race falling into that category was the Olander Park 24-Hour Run, held on a shaded 1.09-mile asphalt path around a beautiful lake in Sylvania, Ohio. Race Director Tom Falvey had the unique ability of making everyone feel like a champion: The runner who completed 50 miles in 24 hours was given the same accolades as the winner who ran more than 150. Over time the number of entrants no longer supported the expenses for conducting the 24-Hour Run, so in 2003 it was turned into a 100-Mile event. I ran it twice more and then—in the blink of an eye—it was gone. However, the memories remain. In its 24-hour format, completing one hundred and twenty-nine miles in 2002 which helped me land an invitation to the 2003 Badwater Ultramarathon. As a 100-mile event, running with my friend Gary Griffin in 2004 and seeing him finish his first 100-miler, and then Gary and I running it again in 2005 where we both saw mutual friend Susan Lance finish *her* first 100-miler.

The second race that fell by the wayside was the Atlanta Marathon. Since 1981 I had spent every Thanksgiving morning lining up for 'the South's oldest marathon' until it was taken away—cold turkey, no less—in 2010. Out of respect I ran the marathon course on Thanksgiving morning for several more years after that until I grew weary of running on a route filled with nonchaperoned holiday morning traffic in busy downtown Atlanta.

Last year I said my goodbyes to the good people at Brooks Elementary School in Brooks, Georgia as their PTO put on the 31ˢᵗ and final edition of the Brooks Day 10K. I'll miss so much about this quaint little race held in conjunction with the Brooks Day Festival on the second Saturday in May: Walking the halls of the school to use the restroom one last time before the race and seeing all the students' drawings and paintings proudly displayed on the bulletin boards, attending the awards presentation and listening for the names of the runners I ran with every weekend as they were called to the main stage to receive their awards, and heading over to the festivities in the park afterwards to watch the youngsters play T-Ball while enjoying a hot, fresh funnel cake courtesy of one of the local merchants.

This December I'll be heading down to the Florida panhandle to run in the Tallahassee Ultra Distance Classic (TUDC). Next year the race moves to a new venue and I want to enjoy the cozy confines of Wakulla Springs State Park—where it's been held since I fell in love with it the very first time I ran it back in 1998—one last time. The quiet seclusion and natural beauty the park offers will take a back seat on the second Saturday in December however, because that's when the ultrarunning community gathers in Wakulla for its annual family reunion and 'run through the jungle' (as the event has been called in recent years) for the last time.

In my 17-year love affair with the TUDC the event has been directed by two husband-and-wife teams whose organization and attention to detail is surpassed only by their commitment to the sport of running and shared passion for making sure each and every runner has the best ultra experience possible. (On how many race applications have you been asked to name your favorite aid station refreshments?) I was welcomed to Wakulla by then-Race Directors Fred and Margaret Deckert that first time and when the event was passed along to current Race Directors Gary and Peg Griffin (that would be the same Gary Griffin who ran his first 100-miler with me back in 2004), I'm happy to report nothing was lost in translation. (Next year when the torch is passed along to Jeff and JoLena Bryan I trust that will be the case as well.) The TUDC remains a first-class event, but more importantly is continues to be a family affair.

The host Gulf Winds Track Club always has plenty of members on hand to provide support. Enthusiastically calling our your name as you finish a *lap and meticulously notating your split time on a clipboard, carefully filling your bottle full of your favorite sports drink or enthusiastically running a lap with you because you need an emotional lift, they do it all. Hot soup, free massages and awards created by local artists are available after you've finished with your 50-kilometers or 50-miles (your choice!). From my personal experience—10 trips to Wakulla and almost 400 miles of running—I can honestly say I've never made a request that wasn't granted (including the year I asked a volunteer to take down my Darkside Running Club banner because I'd just spent more than eight hours running 50-miles in monsoon conditions and 41-degree temperatures).

*Originally one lap was an intimate 2.07-mile route through the park. In 2010 it was modified to a 10-kilometer route, much of it outside of the confines of Wakulla Springs State Park.

The Tallahassee Ultra Distance Classic has a storied history (do yourself a favor and research it on the internet when you have some time) and is the proud home of numerous record-setting performances and countless first-time ultra finishers. On a personal level I've forged many personal relationships at Wakulla that have stood the test of time as well as the endless miles we've run together over the years.

I have many fond memories of my 10 trips to Wakulla Springs State Park. When I return to the Wakulla Lodge this year to run the TUDC one last time I have no doubt that each and every one of them will run through my mind at some point during the weekend (I always make the TUDC a weekend adventure, driving down on Friday and driving home on Sunday).

The memory that stands out most is that second Saturday in December in 2007. I had just lost both of my parents within a period of six weeks prior to the TUDC and thought--although I wasn't particularly keen on running 31 miles—that being around some familiar faces would do me good. Fifteen minutes prior to the start, Race Director Gary gave his usual spirited and motivational pre-race speech and ended it by dedicating the race to the memories of my mom and dad. Then once the race began I ran the first couple of laps with Amy Costa, who offered me an eight-mile-per-hour shoulder to lean on as she spoke about how much her father meant to her before transitioning to asking me questions about my parents. I couldn't have paid for better therapy.

Come to find out I was exactly right: Being around some familiar faces did me good.

Especially when the familiar faces are family.

Postscript: After the race Co-Race Director Gary Griffin sent the following message:

At the onset of the race last Saturday it seemed that this would be the final Tallahassee Ultra Distance Classic to ever take place at the hallowed venue of Wakulla Springs State Park. But while you were out there running, something quite unexpected and wonderfully exciting happened...your basic Christmas miracle, if you will. Nancy Stedman and Jay Silvania, the outgoing and longtime RD's of the Tallahassee Marathon, offered to assume directorship of the 2015 TUDC at Wakulla Springs. Jeff and JoLena Bryan, who were the Gulf Winds Track Club Board-approved RD's for the 2015 TUDC will now become the RD's of a local 8-hour run in 2015 at a place and date to be determined. This is all subject to Board approval but at this point it certainly appears as though the long history of the TUDC at Wakulla Springs on the 2nd Saturday in December will continue!

Footnote: When I posted my 'Last Call at Wakulla' story on my Facebook page the first one to 'like' it was Jay Silvania. My work is done.

THE TIME IS NOW

———— ∞∞ ————

November 29, 1978.

People were anxious to see what JR would do next on *Dallas*.

Lord of the Rings—the **original** *Lord of the Rings*—was ruling the box office.

Donna Summer's *MacArthur Park* was in heavy rotation on the radio and all of the popular discotheques (Yes, you heard me: Discotheques!).

A new car sold for $6,400 and its 16-gallon gas tank could be filled for a little over $10.

I had been married a little over a year, attending graduate school at the University of Florida, living in married student housing and teaching two public speaking courses to undergraduates. Lou Ann Fernald was in my first period class (more on that later).

November 29, 1978. It was also the last day I didn't run.

I started running every day on Thursday, November 30, 1978—less than two weeks before I took my oral exams for my Master's degree with the two professors who had gotten me interested in running several months earlier. I didn't run the previous day because I spent the day in the bathroom, the result of winning a bet with one of my professors. The bet?

Me: *I can run 13 miles.*

Professor: *No you can't.*

I won the bet. That is, if you consider running 13 miles for the first time and then spending the next day never more than 20 feet away from the toilet because your stomach felt as if it had been mauled by a Grizzly Bear as 'winning,' then yes: I won the bet.

Today is Sunday, November 30, 2014. I'll be turning 60 in 10 days. I've been pounding the pavement to the tune of 137,000 miles over the past 36 years. There was actually a 16-year period of time in my life when I averaged a half marathon a day. OK, I admit a minor addiction to running lots and lots of miles and have resolved each of the last 20 years to cut back (without fail, I might add), but today I'm going to do something about it.

After all, 36 years of averaging more than 10 miles a day and knocking on the door of my 60th birthday is as good a time as any to start thinking about some of the things I want to be able to do in the years ahead, such as:

- Negotiate the stairs down to the basement and up to the bonus room on the second level of our new home.

- Chase my grandson through the woods, up and down the driveway and all around the back yard.

- Carry a 42-pound bag of kitty litter from the trunk of the car to the basement.

- Rake almost two acres' worth of leaves in the fall.

- Roll a full garbage can down our 300-foot long driveway every Tuesday morning, and then pull the empty garbage can back *up* the driveway on Tuesday afternoon.

You get the idea.

Scott Ludwig

Long story short: My body is tired. Once the sun goes down—whether its daylight saving time or not—I'm ready to call it a day and turn in for the night. Sad but true.

So today is the beginning of the New Me. I'm not going to feel compelled to run nine or 10 miles every weekday. I won't feel obligated to run considerably longer distances on weekends. I'm not...I won't...I'm ready to **JUST SAY NO** to high mileage.

Now if you'll excuse me, I have to ask the Old Me to explain to the New Me why 'we' ran 13 miles this morning. Once We're both on the same page I know We'll be just fine. Starting tomorrow.

Getting back to Lou Ann Fernald, six months after taking my class she went on to bigger and better things as _Playboy_ magazine's Miss June 1979.

As for me, it's now 36 years later and my body has never graced the pages of _Runner's World_.

But there's always tomorrow.

EPILOGUE

My wife gave me a book for Christmas: *Aging Gracefully* by Linda Staten and Jeannie Hund. This came about 10 days after I wrote Chapter 50 of this book with the same title (the chapter, not the book).

In the book I found this:

> *There is a certain age when society begins to refer to us as 'mature,' which only proves once again that society doesn't have a clue.*

I'd like to think I said the exact same thing in my book,

Only with a lot more words.

Celebrating the end of my 60-mile 60th birthday run the only way I know how

This would almost have you believing I'm a Baltimore Ravens fan (I'm not)

The complete Scott Ludwig collection (excluding this book, of course)

Be careful when you order a cake from a baker
who attended the University of Georgia

The Senoia Road Six (actually five; Axle was beneath
a car when this picture was taken)

Believe it or not, all mixed drinks at the University
of Florida uses these two ingredients!

Krischan met Danny Wuerffel and they hit it off immediately (not)

My fear of heights would have been obvious had you seen me shaking while
I took this photograph standing on a log three feet above the ground.

Krischan celebrating his first official one-mile race the only way he knows

Alternate author photo (I thought the photo of the dead flowers I chose instead was more indicative of hitting the big SIX-OH)

Reaching the top Siler Bald...with evidence to prove it

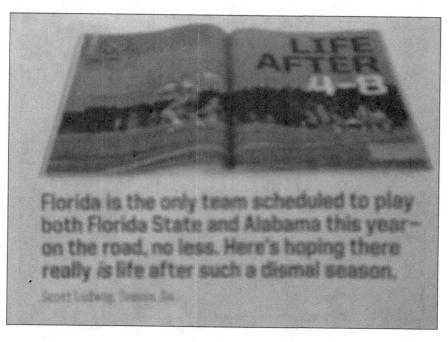

It took more than 40 years to get here (on the pages of Sports Illustrated)

My running route of choice in Pittsburgh (the asphalt, not the water)

Moments before the Baltimore Ravens-Carolina Panthers game. 'Nevermore', qouth the Raven. 'Never again', qouth Scott.

I went all the way to Baltimore so Ray Lewis could tap dance on my head

Krischan was into the holiday spirit so much this year he thought
he was a reindeer. The kid has quite the imagination.

Random photograph of my grandson because everyone should have
one (not your own grandson, but a photo of MY grandson)

No explanation necessary

Taking a short break during my 60-mile birthday run because
the crow asked for one (crows have no endurance)

ACKNOWLEDGEMENTS

———————— ⌘ ————————

I've spent this entire book acknowledging those who may/may not have been accomplices, instigators and/or enablers these past 12 months. That being said there is no need for me to mention their names again. Please know I appreciate everything (and to some of you I expect your total silence about those little things I pointed out as 'unmentionable' and/or 'non-repeatable' throughout the year) and that this book couldn't possibly be complete without mentioning each and every one of you. (Just don't expect me to mention your names because as I already said, there is no need for me to mention your names again.)

As for those of you I haven't mentioned up until now it's time you realized: That ship has sailed.

As for the photographs in this book, they are all from my personal collection compliments of my $99 digital camera, iPad or iPhone. After all, nothing is too good for fine literature. Thanks to Susanne Thurman for converting them to something I could use in this book.

The front cover features my anniversary 'Gator' flowers. The flowers are fresh, vibrant and healthy. Like me many, many years ago. The back cover features the same flowers six months later, Dried up, wilted and old. Sort of like me now.

Rats.